Dialogues and Games of

Volume 1

How to Play Dialogues

An Introduction to Dialogical Logic

Volume 1
How to Play Dialogues: An Introduction to Dialogical Logic
Juan Redmond and Matthieu Fontaine

Dialogues and Games of Logic Series Editors
Shahid Rahman   shahid.rahman@univ-lille3.fr
Nicolas Clerbout
Matthieu Fontaine

How to Play Dialogues

An Introduction to Dialogical Logic

Juan Redmond

and

Matthieu Fontaine

ISBN 978-1-84890-046-2

College Publications
Scientific Director: Dov Gabbay
Managing Director: Jane Spurr
Department of Informatics
King's College London, Strand, London WC2R 2LS, UK

www.collegepublications.co.uk

Original cover design by Laraine Welch
Printed by Lightning Source, Milton Keynes, UK

Dedicated to the memory of our friend Paul Gochet

The following book is an edition of *College Publications* and the research group *Pragmatisme Dialogique* headed by Shahid Rahman at the University of Lille 3 – Charles-de-Gaulle and in collaboration with the laboratory *Savoirs, Textes, Langage* (Unité Mixte de Recherche 8163, Lille 3).

How to play Dialogues constitutes the first introduction to Dialogical Logic aimed at the practice of dialogic containing precise comments on solutions to exercises in first-order classical, intuitionistic and elements of propositional modal logic. It is the first part of the work ***The Dialogues of Logic,*** conceived in two separate autonomous texts on dialogical logic. The two texts should provide together a comprehensive technical and philosophical overview of the dialogical approach to logic.

Table of contents

Foreword

The expression *Dialogical Logic* refers to a research tradition that can be traced back to at least Greek antiquity, when logic was conceived as the systematic study of dialogues in which two parties exchange arguments over a central claim. In its modern form, dialogical logic uses concepts of game theory to design dialogue games that provide semantics for a wide range of logical systems. The modern approach, originally developed in the context of constructive mathematics and logic, has proved to be fruitful for the study, comparison and combination of various logical systems, such as connexive, epistemic dynamic logic, free, modal, paraconsistent, and substructural logics.[1] Dialogical logic also has been recently applied to provide formal reconstructions of the historical development of logic when logic and argumentation were linked by inseparable bonds, such as in the Indian tradition of logic, and in the Arabic and medieval theories of disputation.[2]

In fact, Dialogical Logic developed by Paul Lorenzen and Kuno Lorenz was the result of a solution to some of the problems that arose in Lorenzen' *Operative Logik* (1955).[3] We can not discuss here thoroughly the passage from the operative to the dialogical approach, though as pointed out by Peter Schroeder-Heister, the insights of Operative logic had lasting consequences in the literature on proof-theory and still deserve attention today.[4] Moreover, the notion of *harmony* formulated by the antirealists and particularly by Dag Prawitz has been influenced by Lorenzen's notions of *admissibility*; *eliminability* and *inversion*. However, the dialogical tradition is rather a rupture than a

---

[1] Cf. Keiff 2009.
[2] Fontaine/Gorisse/Rahman 2011: "Dynamique Dialogique: Lecture d'une controverse entre logiciens jaïns et grammairiens en Inde classique", forthcoming in Actes du Colloque "Jeux, Dialogues et Interaction".
[3] Cf. Lorenz 2001.
[4] Schröder-Heister 2008.

continuation of the operative project, and it might be confusing to start by linking conceptually both projects together.

Dialogical Logic was suggested at the end of the 1950s by Paul Lorenzen and then worked out by Kuno Lorenz.[6] Inspired by Wittgenstein's *meaning as use,* the basic idea of the dialogical approach to logic is that the meaning of the logical constants is given by the norms or rules for their use. This feature of its underlying semantics quite often motivated the dialogical approach to be understood as a *pragmatic* approach to meaning. The terminology might be misleading and induce one to think that the theory of meaning involved in dialogic is not semantics at all. The formulation *pragmatist semantics* seems to be more appropriate.

Anyway, the point is that those rules that fix meaning may be of more than one type, and that they determine the kind of reconstruction of an argumentative and/or linguistic practice that a certain kind of language games called dialogues provide. As mentioned above the dialogical approach to logic is not a logic but a semantic rule-based framework where different logics could be developed, combined or compared.

In a dialogue two parties argue about a thesis respecting certain fixed rules. The player that states the thesis is called Proponent (**P**); His rival, who puts into question the thesis, is called Opponent (**O**). In its original form, dialogues were designed in such a way that each of the plays end after a finite number of moves with one player winning, while the other loses. Actions or moves in a dialogue are often understood as *utterances*[7] or as speech-acts[8]. The

---

[6] The main original papers are collected in Lorenzen/Lorenz 1978. A detailed account of recent developments can be found in Felscher 1985, Keiff 2004, Keiff 2007, Rahman 2009, Rahman 2011, Rahman/Keiff 2004, Rahman/Clerbout/Keiff 2009, Keiff 2009, Fiutek/Rukert/Rahman 2010, Rahman/Tulenheimo 2006, Rukert 2001, Rukert 2007. For a textbook presentation (in French), see Fontaine/Redmond 2008.

[7] Cf. Rahman/Rückert 2001, 111 and Rückert 2001, chapter 1.2.

[8] Cf. Keiff 2007.

point is that the rules of the dialogue do not operate on expressions or sentences isolated from the act of uttering them. The rules are divided into particle rules or rules for logical constants (*Partikelregeln*) and structural rules (*Rahmenregeln*). The structural rules determine the general course of a dialogue game, whereas the particle rules regulate those moves (or utterances) that are requests (to the moves of a rival) and those moves that are answers (to the requests).

Crucial for the dialogical approach, and that which distinguishes it from all other approaches, are the following points (which will be developed in the main body of the present book)

- The distinction between local (rules for logical constants) and global meaning (included in the structural rules).
- The symmetry of local meaning. This feature amounts to player independence.
- The distinction between the play level (local winning or winning of a play) and the strategic level (global winning or existence of a winning strategy).

These distinctive features of dialogical logic make it an ideal instrument for the development of a general framework in which argumentative, model theoretic and proof-theoretic approaches to logic can be studied. Indeed, while model-theoretic approaches show their limitations in the context of the logic of bounded resources (linear logic), proof-theoretic approaches can not deal with either incomplete logics or with non-monotonic reasoning.

As mentioned above, very recently dialogical logic had also been shown to be a fruitful instrument for the formal reconstruction of developments in the history of logic - when the dynamic features of argumentation permeated the notion of inference. It is this dynamic spirit of inference well beyond the precincts of truth-theory and proof-theory that we seek to reintroduce in the formal systems of today with the help of a logic that results from the dialogical interaction of human agents.

At this point, I would like to quote the words of John Woods, who in the context of the development of dialogical logic for fiction wrote:

I find this a delightful development, lending desired emphasis to the proposition that when directed to activities performed by actual human agents, a well-made logic is a humanities discipline at least as much as it is a mathematical one. [9]

Shahid Rahman
Université de Lille, UMR: 8163, STL
shahid.rahman@univ-lille3.fr

---

[9] Woods 2011. Report of Redmond's doctorate Thesis.

PROPOSITIONAL DIALOGICAL LOGIC

§1-Language for propositional logic

A vocabulary **L** for propositional logic consists of a set of letters (p, q, r, ...) that stand for the simplest sentences of this formal language, which can be built into complex sentences by means of the connectives: negation "¬", conjunction "∧", disjunction "∨", conditional "→", brackets ")"and "(".

The well-formed formulas of propositional logic are expressions inductively defined as follows:
1. Each propositional letter is, on its own, a wff.
2. If φ is a wff, then $\neg\varphi$ is a wff.
3. If φ and θ are wffs, and "&" is a binary connective, then "$\varphi\&\theta$" is a wff. Here "&" could be "∨", "∧" or "→".
4. Only what can be generated by clauses (1) to (3) in a finite number of steps is a wff.

§2-Language for dialogical propositional logic

We first define the language for propositional dialogical logic (**L$_D$**) as the result of enriching the language of propositional logic (**L**) with the following meta-logical symbols:

    i. two force symbols, **?** and **!**;
    ii. the symbols 1, 2;
    iii. two labels, **O** and **P** (standing for the players, Opponent and Proponent, respectively).

§3-Particle and structural rules

The dialogues are developed using two types of rules. On one hand, *Particle rules* that abstractly describe the way a formula can be attacked and defended, according to its main connective. *Structural rules*, on the other hand, specify the general organization of the game. Let's see now more in detail how the rules work in the dialogical games.

What is a particle rule?

A particle rule describes the way a formula of a given main connective may be objected to, and how to answer the objection. By definition, an argumentation form is a tuple consisting of (1) a formula, (2) a set of *attacks*, (3) a set of *defences*, and (4) a relation specifying for each attack the corresponding defence(s). Argumentation forms are abstract in the sense that, in their definition, no reference is made to the context of argumentation in which the rule is applied. The particle rules thus constitute the *local semantics* of a logic, for they determine the dialogical meaning of each logical constant but say nothing about the way this meaning may be related to anything else.

We can understand these rules supposing that one of the players (**X** or **Y**) asserts a formula which he has to defend against the attacks of the other player (**Y** or **X**, respectively). This formula is either a conjunction or a disjunction or a conditional or a negation or a quantified expression (in first-order logic).

Before presenting the particle rules in §7 we provide some notions that will help us to reach the goal:

§4-Dialogical expressions

To present the rules we will use the following
tripartite or dialogical expressions (Γ and Λ):

dialogical expressions Γ	*dialogical expressions* Λ
X-!-Y and **Y-!-Y**,	**X-?-Ж** and **Y-?-Ж**
X and Y are the players and we assume that X≠Y	

§5-Formulas & target of a question

In the _expressions_ Γ: Ψ is a "formula" and "!" indicates that this formula must be defended.
In the _expressions_ Λ: "?" indicates that the expression is a "question" and $\mathcal{K}$ is the target of the question.

The targets of a question are conjunctions or disjunctions, according to the rules for propositional logic that will be exposed further.

§6-Attacks and defences

A dialogue, after the thesis (a formula), consists of attacks and defences.
Attacks are performed by means of formulas or questions.
Defences are performed only with formulas.

The action of attacking or defending with formulas
will be expressed as _uttering_ formulas.

Uttering and Commitment

Upon _uttering_ a formula (any formula) a player X _commits_ himself to the challenger Y to defend the formula against all attacks allowed to Y.

For every particle there is a special commitment. That is to say, there is a particular commitment depending on the formula uttered (a conjunction, a disjunction, a conditional or negation or an atomic formula).

All dialogues are deployed from the commitments of players with the formulas uttered: the thesis or the formulas uttered for attacking or defending other formulas.

Remember: a question is always an attack but not vice versa.
An attack could be performed by a question or by uttering a formula.
A defence corresponds always to a formula uttered.

X-!-Ψ		
X	**!**	**Ψ**
Player X	The formula Ψ must be defended	Ψ is a formula.
O or P	In general, all tripartite expressions where the symbol "!" occur correspond to a formula that must be defended.	Examples of formulas: ¬A, A∨B, A→B, etc. Where A and B are atomics or complex.

X-?-Ж		
X	**?**	**Ж**
Player X	A question	The target of the question.
O or P		If Ж = ∧₁, then X-?-∧₁ If Ж = ∨, then X-?-∨ The same for the others For first-order logic: Ж =∀x/c (X-?-∀x/c) Ж =∃x (X-?-∃x)

Similarly for **Y-?- Ж** and **Y-!- Ж.**

The moves of **X** and **Y** are performed alternatively. Thus, after the attack or the defence of **X** the respective attack or defence of **Y** will come, and so on (like a play of chess).

In what follows, we will explain how to *attack* and how to *defend* a formula (local semantics). If the formula is complex (a conjunction, etc.), attacks and defences will concern the particles participating in the complex formula (¬, ∨, →, ∧).

§7-Particle Rules

7.1 Rule for the conjunction:

[For the sake of clarity, in the conjunction A∧B we call "A" the first member and "B" the second member of the conjunction]

∧		
Formula uttered	Attack	Defence
A∧B	A question: ?	A or B A formula which must be defended: "!"
dialogical expressions:		
X-!-A∧B	Y-?-∧₁ Y-?-∧₂ ∧₁: left side of the conjunction ∧₂: right side of the conjunction **Y** has the choice	X-!-A X-!-B

Explanation

X utters the conjunction A∧B which must be defended (!) Punctually, the player **X** commits himself to uttering each member of the formula if the challenger requires it. How does one attack this formula? Since **X** commits himself to the utterance of each member, then the challenger **Y** has the right to decide which one of the members the player **X** should utter. There are two <u>nonexclusive</u> possibilities: either **Y** asks (?) for the first member of the conjunction (**Y**-?-∧₁), or **Y** asks for the second (**Y**-?-∧₂). The defence consists of uttering – when it is possible – the first member (**X**-!-A) or the second member (**X**-!-B), respectively. After the last movement, the player **X** must defend A and B separately.

7.2 Rule for the disjunction:

[For the sake of clarity, in the disjunction A∨B we call "A" the first member and "B" the second member of the disjunction]

∨		
Formula uttered	Attack	Defence
A∨B	A question: ?	A or B A formula which must be defended: "!"
dialogical expressions:		
X-!-A∨B	**Y**-?-∨ **X** has the choice	**X**-!-A or **X**-!-B

Explanation

X utters the disjunction A∨B, which must be defended (!) Punctually, the player **X** commits himself to uttering at least one of the two members of the disjunction. How does one attack this formula? Challenger **Y** requests player **X** to utter at least one of the two members (Y-?-∨). Since **X** commits himself to the utterance of at least one of the members without specifying which one, **X** concedes **Y** the possibility to choose: **X** defends the disjunction either uttering the formula of the left side (**X**-!-A) or the formula of the right side (**X**-!-B). After the last movement, the player **X** must defend A and B separately if that is required by the challenger.

7.3 Rule for the conditional:

[For the sake of clarity, in the conditional A→B we call "A" the first member and "B" the second member of the conditional]

→		
Formula uttered	Attack	Defence
A→B	A A formula	B A formula which must be defended: "!"

dialogical expressions:		
X-!-A→B	**Y**-!-A	**X**-!-B

Explanation:
"Hic Rodhus, hic salta"

X utters the conditional A→B, which must be defended (!) Punctually, the player **X** commits himself at uttering B if the challenger concedes to utter A. How does one challenge this utterance? Challenger **Y** concedes the first member uttering A (**Y**-!-A). The defence of **X** consists on uttering B, the second member of the conditional: (**X**-!-B). After the last movement, the player **X** must defend B.

Note that there is another possibility to respond to the challenge of **Y** that will be developed later (see XXX).

7.4 Rule for the negation:

¬		
Formula uttered	Attack	Defence
¬A	A A formula	Not defence
dialogical expressions:		
X-!- ¬A	**Y**-!-A	----------

Explanation

X utters a negated formula ¬A, which must be defended (!) How does one challenge this formula? By uttering the opposite "A": (**Y**-!-A). There is no defence for this attack. After the last movement, the player **X** must defend A.

Summary 1

		Formula	Attack	Defence
i	∧	X-!-A∧B	Y-?-∧$_1$ Y-?-∧$_2$ <small>Y has the choice</small>	X-!-A X-!-B
ii	∨	X-!-A∨B	Y-?-∨	X-!-A or X-!-B <small>X has the choice</small>
iii	→	X-!-A→B	Y-!-A	X-!-B
iv	¬	X-!-¬A	Y-!-A	No defence

At this point it is important to maintain the distinction between
formula, question, attack and *defence*
For this purpose we will use different verbs:
to attack, to respond and to defend

To attack and *to respond* are the actions that a player performs against the formulas already uttered by the other player: column "Attack" in the rules (see Summary 1).

To defend means to utter a formula corresponding to the column "Defence" in the Rules (see Summary 1).

"To attack" differs from "to respond" in that the latter is the attack performed after an attack not already defended by the other player. (See as example "particle rule for conditional")

We never attack a question; attacks are only over formulas. We can attack a formula either by uttering a formula or performing a question. We defend a formula from an attack only by uttering a formula. It is possible to respond to an attack with another attack; however, in this case the first attack still remains without defence.

Summary 2

	Formula	Question
To attack	×	×
To respond	×	×
To defend	×	

To attack=To respond
To defend=To utter a formula

It is worth noting that an expression like X-!-A (A=formula) without any other explanation could be either an attack, a defence, or even a response. That's the reason why we need <u>extra information</u> to be more specific in order to explain a developing dialogue. Therefore, we introduce in the next section the *role* of a player.

§8-State of a dialogue

In what follows, we will describe the development of a dialogue using the concept of *State of a dialogue*. A State of a dialogue is a pair <ρ, Φ> in which:

ρ is the role of a player, either *challenger* or *defender*. The challenger X or Y challenges or attacks formulas of the other player with a question (?) or by uttering a formula (!). On the contrary, a defence is always a formula uttered (!).

> Role of challenger= **CH**
> Role of defender= **D**

Φ: is a *dialogical expression* (Γ or Λ): (**X-!-Ψ, Y-!-Ψ, X-?-Ж and Y-?-Ж**).

State of a dialogue & Move

A State of a dialogue describes a *move*.
All dialogues begin with the thesis. Therefore, it is the only move without a specific role.

Summary 2

Examples of moves (by means of "states of dialogue")		
$<CH, \text{Y-?-}\wedge_2>$	$< CH, \text{Y-!-A}>$	$< D, \text{X-!-A}>$
The player Y performs an attack (CH) with a question (?) whose target is $\wedge_2$.	The player Y performs an attack (CH) uttering a formula A that must be defended (!)	The player X performs a defence (D) uttering a formula A that must be defended (!)

Therefore, it is through "states of a dialogue" that we will detail the moves of a dialogue. However, before we need the following definitions:

[**Definition 1**]: *Move* → A formula uttered or a question performed by a player

Remark: Players make their moves alternately. (After **X** moves, **Y** follows, etc.) Every move is numbered. The thesis has the number 0, and so on.

[**Definition 2**]: *Play* → Set of moves.

[**Definition 3**]: *Round* → attack+defense.

[**Definition 4**]: *Game* → Set of plays in a finished dialogue which begin with the thesis. Every game is a play but not the opposite. The number of games is n+1, where n=number of branches (In fact, branching might be seen as a notion that corresponds to the level of strategies rather than to the level of plays (see discussion in Appendix).

§9-States of dialogue for every particle

In what follows we present the particle rules by means of "states of dialogue".

Note: For the moment we set aside whether the beginning of a play – a formula which must be defended – corresponds to an attack or a defence.

9.1 Particle rule for Negation (N):

The play begins with a negated formula, i.e., $\Psi = \neg\mathbf{A}$.
The play is composed by moves N_i ($N_i = N_1$, and N_2).

Players	dialogical expressions	Explanations
X	Move N_1= <--, X-!-¬A>	X utters the formula ¬A and must defend it (!)
Y	Move N_2= < *CH*, Y-!-A>	Y attacks (*CH*) with the opposite formula "A" and then must defend it (!).
X		No defence

9.2 Particle rule for conjunction (C):

The play begins with a conjunction, e.g., $\Psi = \mathbf{A}\wedge\mathbf{B}$.
The play is composed of moves C_i ($C_i = C_1$, C_2 and C_3).

Players	dialogical expressions	Explanations
X	Move C_1=<-,X-!-A∧B>	X utters the formula A∧B and must defend it (!)
Y	Move C_2=< *CH*,Y-?-∧₁> / <?,Y-?-∧₂>	Y attacks (*CH*) by asking (?) for a justification of the left/right member of the conjunction, i.e., **Y-?-∧₁ / Y-?-∧₂**. The expressions ∧₁ and ∧₂ are the targets of the question. It is possible to ask for both subsequently.
X	Move C_3=< *D*, X-!-A> / < *D*, X-!-B>	The defence (*D*) of X consists of uttering the right or the left member of the conjunction A or B respectively. These lasts formulas must be defended (!).

9.3 Particle rule for disjunction (D):

The play begins with a disjuntion, e.g., A∨B.
The play is composed of moves D_i ($D_i = D_1$, D_2 and D_3).

Players	dialogical expressions	Explanations
X	Move D_1=<–,X-!-A∨B>	X utters the formula A∨B and must defend it (!)
Y	Move D_2=< *CH*,Y-?-∨>	Y attacks (*CH*) by asking (?) for at least one of the two members of the disjunction.
X	Move D_3=< *D*, X-!-A>/< *D*, X-!-B>	The defence (*D*) of X consists of uttering at least one of the two members of the disjunction, A or B. These last formulas must be defended (!)

9.4 Particle rule for Conditional (I):

The play begins with a conditional, e.g., A→B.
The play is composed of moves I_i ($I_i = I_1$, I_2 and I_3).

Players	dialogical expressions	Explanations
X	Move I_1=<–,X-!-A→B>	X utters the formula A→B and must defend it (!)
Y	Move I_2=< *CH*,Y-!-A>	Y attacks (*CH*) by conceding A. This last formula must be defended (!)
X	Move I_3=< *D*, X-!-B>	The defence (*D*) of X consists of uttering B. This last formula must be defended (!)
Note that if A (in move I_2) is a complex formula (negation, conjunction, disjunction or conditional), X can *respond* (see summary XXX) – before move I_3 – by attacking move I_2 with a formula or a question according to N_2, C_2, D_2 or I_2 respectively.		

Summary 3

Every move is described by an ordered pair called *State of dialogue*

State of dialogue=<ρ, Φ>

Φ = P-!-Ψ, O-!-Ψ, P-?- Ж et O-?- Ж

Ψ for the first move: ¬A, A∧B, A∨B, A→B

Ψ for the second move corresponding to N_2, C_2, etc.

Ж is the target of a question and is always an attack.

For reading

Expressions	In the same order:
< *CH*, Y-!-A>	<Attack, player Y, defends, formula A>
< *D*, X-!-B>	<Defence, player X, defends, formula B>
< *CH*, X-?-(∧₁/∧₂/∨)>	<Attack, player X, questions, target>

From now on, players will take a specific role in a dialogue. There are two roles to interpret depending on the player who uttered the thesis. Note that the thesis is the beginning of a dialogue, and thus the roles of players will not change thereafter. The player who uttered the thesis is the *Proponent*; the other player is the *Opponent*. Both will take the role of challenger, attacking each other depending on the particular development of each dialogue.

Attacks and defences will constitute the plot of all the dialogues.

The sequence of attacks and defences can not go beyond atomic formulas.

§10-Dialogues in action: An illustration (choices and branching)

Dialogues are developed in a frame with two main columns, one for each player. Each move has a number that will be indicated to the left and to the right of each column.

	O			P	
				Thesis	0
1					2
3					4
5					...

In general, after uttering the thesis, the Proponent (**P**) must be able to resist all possible attacks allowed (especially by the particle rules) to the Opponent (**O**). One of the most important devices in the context of the definition of a winning strategy for the **P** is *branching* that guarantees that all possible responses of the Opponent have been considered. Indeed, branching makes possible to display all parallel plays that cover all the possibilities. In fact, branching seems to have a stratetegic underpinning built on top of the level of plays (see discussion in Appendix).

Players, choices and branching[10]

Branching is the result of players' choices in a dialogue. So far, we have not made any difference between X and Y relating to choices, and the role of proponent or opponent in a dialogue. But from now on it will be of great importance to know if the choices corresponding to the particles ($\neg$, $\vee$, $\rightarrow$, $\wedge$) belong to **O** or **P**.

Thus, in addition to the particle rules, we will consider branching according to the following definition:

---

[10] See Appendix

[Definition 6]: Branching

Only the Opponent (O) implements branchings in a dialogue. O implements branchings, in relation to the choices made, in the following cases:

(i)   O defends a disjunction (see branching for D_3),
(ii)   O attacks a conjunction (see branching for C_2),
(iii)   O defends a conditional (see branching for I_3).

Branching is a structural rule and will be presented again below.

Let's see below some examples of generic dialogues where the difference between O and P is at stake:

❧ 10.1-Illustration for negation ❧

In every case we analyze the two cases: X=P and X=O

(A) If X=P

	O			P	
				¬A	N_1
N_2	A				

Where the moves are described as follows:

$$N_1 = <\text{--}, P\text{-}!\text{-}\neg A>$$
$$N_2 = < CH, O\text{-}!\text{-}A>$$

(B) If X=O

	O			P	
N_1	¬A				
				A	N_2

Moves:

$$N_1 = <\text{--}, O\text{-}!\text{-}\neg A>$$
$$N_2 = < CH, P\text{-}!\text{-}A>$$

❧ 10.2-Illustration for conjunction ❧

(A) If X=P Branching in C_2 (Definition 6, *ii*)

	O			P	
				$A \wedge B$	C_1

↙ ↘

Branch 1

	O			P	
				$A \wedge B$	C_1
C_2	$?-\wedge_1$			A	C_3

Moves

$C_1 = <\text{--}, \text{P-!-}A \wedge B>$

$C_2 = <\boldsymbol{CH}, \text{O-?-}\wedge_1>$

$C_3 = <\boldsymbol{D}, \text{P-!-A}>$

Branch 2

	O			P	
				$A \wedge B$	C_1
$C_{2'}$	$?-\wedge_2$			B	$C_{3'}$

Moves

$C_1 = <\text{--}, \text{P-!-}A \wedge B>$

$C_{2'} = <\boldsymbol{CH}, \text{O-?-}\wedge_2>$

$C_{3'} = <\boldsymbol{D}, \text{P-!-B}>$

Both branches must be played

— • —

(B) If X=O (no branching, two options, P decides)

Option 1

	O			P	
C_1	$A \wedge B$				
C_3	A			$?-\wedge_1$	C_2

Option 2

	O			P	
C_1	$A \wedge B$				
$C_{3'}$	B			$?-\wedge_2$	$C_{2'}$

Details

Option 1	$C_1 = <\text{--}, \text{O-!-}A \wedge B>$
	$C_2 = <\boldsymbol{CH}, \text{P-?-}\wedge_1>$
	$C_3 = <\boldsymbol{D}, \text{O-!-A}>$
Option 2	$C_1 = <\text{--}, \text{O-!-}A \wedge B>$
	$C_{2'} = <\boldsymbol{CH}, \text{P-?-}\wedge_2>$
	$C_{3'} = <\boldsymbol{D}, \text{O-!-B}>$

The proponent can choose any of the two options or both, depending on the strategy played. At the moment a *strategy* is the way a player decides how to perform the attacks (questions or uttering formulas) and defences (uttering formulas) to achieve the goal: to win the dialogue.

❧ 10.3-Illustration for disjunction ❧

(A) If X=P (no branching, two options, P decides)

<table>
<tr><td colspan="3" align="center">Option 1</td><td colspan="3" align="center">Option 2</td></tr>
<tr><td colspan="2" align="center">O</td><td colspan="2" align="center">P</td><td colspan="2" align="center">O</td><td colspan="2" align="center">P</td></tr>
<tr><td></td><td></td><td>A∨B</td><td>D₁</td><td></td><td></td><td>A∨B</td><td>D₁</td></tr>
<tr><td>D₂</td><td>?-∨</td><td>A</td><td>D₃</td><td>D₂</td><td>?-∨</td><td>B</td><td>D₃'</td></tr>
</table>

	Details
Option 1	D₁=<--, P-!-A∨B>
	D₂=< *CH,* O-?-∨>
	D₃=< *D*, P-!-A>
Option 2	D₁=<--, P-!-A∨B>
	D₂=< *CH,* O-?-∨>
	D₃'=< *D*, P-!-B>

The proponent can choose any of the two options or both, depending on the strategy played.

– • –

(B) If X=O Branching in D₃ (Definition 6, *i*)

<table>
<tr><td></td><td colspan="2" align="center">O</td><td></td><td colspan="2" align="center">P</td><td></td></tr>
<tr><td>D₁</td><td>A∨B</td><td></td><td></td><td></td><td></td><td></td></tr>
<tr><td></td><td></td><td></td><td></td><td>?-∨</td><td>D₂</td><td></td></tr>
<tr><td></td><td></td><td></td><td></td><td></td><td></td><td></td></tr>
</table>

↙ ↘

Branch 1						Branch 2				
O			P			O			P	
D_1	A∨B					D_1	A∨B			
D_3	A			?-∨	D_2	$D_{3'}$	B		?-∨	D_2

Moves	Moves
D_1=<--, O-!-A∨B>	D_1=<--, O-!-A∨B>
D_2=< **CH**, P-?-∨>	D_2=< **CH**, P-?-∨>
D_3=< **D**, O-!-A>	$D_{3'}$=< **D**, O-!-B>

Both branches must be played

❧ 10.4-Illustration for the conditional ❧

(A) If X=P (no branching, two options)

Option 1						Option 2				
O			P			O			P	
			A→B	I_1					A→B	I_1
I_2	A		B	I_3		I_2	A			
									Attack A	$I_{3'}$

Details	
Option 1	I_1=<--, P-!-A→B>
	I_2=< **CH**, O-!-A>
	I_3=< **D**, P-!-B>
Option 2	I_1=<--, P-!-A→B>
	I_2=< **CH**, O-!-A>
	$I_{3'}$=< **CH**, (attacks D_2, C_2, N_2 or I_2)>

The proponent can choose one of the two options or both, depending on the strategy played. Option 2 is allowed principally when A is a complex formula (disjunction, conjunction, negation or conditional), or if in the dialogue there are other complex formulas to attack. For the sake of simplicity, we will call "attacks 2" the attacks D_2, C_2, N_2, or I_2.

$$- \bullet -$$

(B) If X=O (branching in I_3, Definition 6, *iii*)

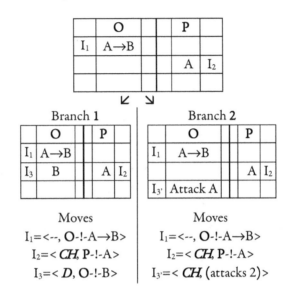

	O			P	
I_1	A→B				
				A	I_2

Branch 1					
	O		P		
I_1	A→B				
I_3	B		A	I_2	

Branch 2					
	O		P		
I_1	A→B				
			A	I_2	
$I_{3'}$	Attack A				

Moves

$I_1 =$ <--, O-!-A→B>

$I_2 =$ < *CH*, P-!-A>

$I_3 =$ < *D*, O-!-B>

Moves

$I_1 =$ <--, O-!-A→B>

$I_2 =$ < *CH*, P-!-A>

$I_{3'} =$ < *CH*, (attacks 2)>

Both branches must be played

Attack 2 is a special case of responding to an attack ("to respond") by attacking, because it is directed towards A (Attack A).

§11-The conditional and the two options of the Opponent: *to respond* and *to defend* an attack

After the attack of a conditional (see 10.4), the Opponent has two options: (i) to *defend* itself from the attack (branch 1) or (ii) to *respond* to the attack (branch 2).

(i) to *defend* itself from an attack of the kind D_2, C_2, $C_{2'}$ or I_2 means to perform the followings moves: D_3, C_3, $C_{3'}$ and I_3 (not $I_{3'}$) respectively.

(ii) *to respond* to an attack means that one must dispense temporarily of (i) and react by attacking the formula already uttered by the other player or by attacking other complex formulas presents in the dialogue. Particularly in the case where X=O we have:

$$\text{To defend: } I_3 = < \boldsymbol{D}, \text{ O-!-B}>$$
$$\text{To respond: } I_{3'} = < \boldsymbol{CH}, (\text{"Attack 2"})>$$

The difference between X=P and X=O is that in the latter case we must develop the two options (branching).

There are other cases besides the conditional where any of the players can *respond* to an attack. In fact, this is one of the most performed strategies when the player cannot *defend* itself immediately. The strategy consists of seeking the formula needed from the utterances of the challenger. More details below.

§12-Structural rules

The *structural rules* establish the general organization of the dialogue. What is at stake in a dialogue is to decide if there is a *wining strategy* for the thesis or not. The aim of the structural rules is to provide a method of decision. The dialogue begins with the thesis. The thesis is the first formula uttered by the proponent and must be defended against all possible attacks allowed to the opponent.

12.1-Proponent and winning strategy

If the *Proponent* succeeds in defending the thesis against all attacks allowed to the challenger, there is a winning strategy for the formula.

The structural rules are chosen in a way that the proponent succeeded defending his thesis against all Opponent attacks if and only if there is a winning strategy for the thesis. We will also see that different types of dialogues can have different types of structural rules.

Note that the dialogues are based on the assumption that each player always follows the best possible strategy.

12.2-Rules

(SR-0) (*Start*): The expressions of a dialogue are numbered, and are alternately asserted by **P** and **O**. The thesis carries the number 0 and is asserted by **P**. All moves after the thesis obey particle and structural rules. We will call D(A) a dialogue D that starts with the thesis A. The even moves (2, 4, ...) are moves made by **P**; the odd moves (1, 3, ...) are made by **O**.

(SR-1 intuitionistic) (*Intuitionistic round closure rule*)
Whenever player **X** is to play, he can attack any move of **Y** in so far as the other rules let him do so, or defend against the *last* attack of **Y**, provided he has not already defended against it. A player may postpone a defence as long as there are attacks that can be put forth.

Example: consider Y=**O** and X=**P**

	O		P	
l	Attack 1		Without answer	
m	Attack 2		Without answer	
			After the move m, **P** can only defend itself from the Attack 2 (never from Attack 1).	

(SR-1 classical) (*Classical round closing rule*)

Whenever player **X** is to play, he can attack any move of **Y** in so far as the other rules let him do so, or defend against *any* attack of **Y** (even the ones against which he has already defended). In other terms, players can play again earlier defences (which makes sense when another move is available).

(SR-2) (*Branching*)

There are three cases in which a dialogue will be extended in such a way that it will generate two distinct (new) games (see definition 4), called dialogical games. These cases are when **O** defends a disjunction (see 10.3 **(B)**), **O** attacks a conjunction (see 10.2 **(A)**), or **O** reacts to an attack against a conditional (see 10.4 **(B)**).

Summary 5

Moves Beginning with:	Branching
$C_1 = <-, P-!-A \wedge B>$	$C_2 = < CH, O-?-\wedge_1 >$ and $C_{2'} = < CH, O-?-\wedge_2 >$
$D_1 => < -, O-!-A \vee B >, D_2 = < CH, P-?-\vee >$	$D_3 = <!, O-!-A >$ and $D_{3'} = <!, O-!-B >$
$I_1 = < -, O-!-A \rightarrow B >$ $I_2 = <?, P-!-A >$	$I_3 = <!, O-!-B >$ and $I_{3'} = < CH, O-\text{"attacks 2"} >$
"attacks 2" = the attacks $(D_2, C_2, N_2$ or $I_2)$	

Note: in a branched dialogue, having a winning strategy for the thesis means that the Proponent wins every dialogical game (every branch) (recall that, as mentioned before, branching relates to the notion of winning strategy - see Appendix).

(SR-3) (*Formal use of atomic formulae*)
Atomic formulas (formulas without connectors or particles) can be uttered *for the first time* only by **O**. The proponent (**P**) can utter an atomic formula only if the same formula was already uttered by **O**. Atomic formulae cannot be attacked.

(SR-4) (*Winning rule for plays*): **finished, open** and **closed** dialogues
- A dialogue is *closed* if and only if the same atomic formula appears in two subsequently positions, one uttered by X and the other by Y. Otherwise the dialogue is still *open* (i.e. no two positions feature the same atomic formula).

Example of a *closed* dialogue:

	O			P	
				Thesis	
l	...				
m	...			...	*n*
s	p			...	*t*
				p	*u*

p= atomic formula

- The player who utters the thesis *wins* if and only if the dialogue is closed. A dialogue is *finished* if and only if it is closed or there is no further move to make according to the rules. The opponent wins if and only if the dialogue is finished and open.

<u>Finished and Closed: **P** wins</u>

Example:

	O			P	
				Thesis	
l	...				
s	p			...	*t*
				p	*u*

Finished and Open: **O** wins

Example:

	O		**P**	
			Thesis	
l	...			
s	p		...	*t*

To introduce the next rule we define first the concept of *repetition*:

(Definition 7) [*Strict repetition of an attack or a defence*]
(i) We speak of a strict repetition of an <u>attack</u> if a move is being attacked although the same move has already been challenged with the same attack before. (Notice that even though choosing the same constant is a strict repetition, the choices of ?-$\wedge_1$ and ?-$\wedge_2$ are in this context different attacks.)

(ii) We speak of a strict repetition of a <u>defence</u> if a challenging move "attack m_1", which has already been defended with the defensive move m_2 before, is being defended against the challenge m_1 once more with the same defensive move. (Notice that the left part and the right part of a disjunction are in this context two different defences.)

(SR-5) (*No delaying tactics rule*)

A non- delaying rule should assure that plays are finite (though there might an infinite number of them). There are several formulations of it with different advantages and disadvantages. The original formulation of Lorenz made use of the notion of *rank* (i.e. a number of challenges and defences allowed in each play and chosen by the players). Other formulations of dialogical logic introduce explicit restrictions on repetitions. Ranks seem to be more compatible with the general aim of the dialogical approach of distinguishing between the play level and the strategic level. Other non-repetition rules seem to presuppose the strategic level.

The following *no-repetition rule* applies to both classical and intuitionistic logic.

> After the move that sets the thesis, and befote starting the gameplayers **O** and **P** each choose a natural number n and m respectively (termed their repetition ranks). Thereafter the players move alternately, each move being a request or an answer.

> In the course of the dialogue, **O** (**P**) may attack or defend any single (token of an) utterance at most n (or m) times and in agreement with SR-1.[11]

The remark on "the agreement with SR-1" is important for intuitionistic logic. The Proponent might well have chosen rank 2. However, SR-1 disallows him to defend twice.

In all of the examples of the book we will assume that the Opponent has chosen rank 1 and the Proponent rank 2. In fact it can be proven that **O** will not improve his chances by choosing a higher rank than 1 (Clerbout [2011]). More generally, because of the undecidabiliy of first-order-logic[12], there is no uniform rank for the proponent that suffices to deliver a decission method for every formula. However, every play will be finite (because the rank is) though the number of plays might be infinite.

(**Definition 8**) [*Winning strategy*]

---

[11] Nicolas Clerbout [2011] proved soundness and completeness of dialogues for first-order logic for a dialogical framework that makes use of the notion of ranks.

[12] A logical system is decidable if there is an effective method for determining whether arbitrary formulas are theorems of the logical system. For example, propositional logic is decidable, because the truth-table method can be used to determine whether an arbitrary propositional formula is logically valid. First-order-logic is not decidable in general, in particular, the set of logical validities in any language for First Order Logic that includes equality and at least one other predicate with two or more arguments is not decidable.

The thesis *A* has a *dialogically winning strategy* in the classical or intuitionistic sense if and only if all games belonging to the respective dialogue are closed.

§13-Intuitionistic and classical logic: How does one play?

Provided that the intuitionistic logic is a conservative restriction of classical logic, all formulas with an *intuitionistic winning strategy* have a *winning strategy* in *classical* logic (but not vice versa). Therefore, we will start the dialogue always from the intuitionistic rules: If the proponent (**P**) wins the formula has a winning strategy in intuitionistic and classical logic. If the proponent loses we continue the dialogue with the classical rules; if the proponent wins this time the formula has a winning strategy only in classical logic (not in intuitionistic logic).

The symbols ☺ and ● will be placed in the end of the dialogue to indicate where the dialogue finishes and which one of the players wins. If there is almost one branching we will find more than one of these symbols.

The symbol ☺ concerns the intuitionistic rules:
SR-0, SR-1$_{\text{intuitionistic}}$, SR-2, SR-3, SR-4, SR-5.

The symbol ● concerns the classical rules:
SR-0, SR-1$_{\text{classical}}$, SR-2, SR-3, SR-4, SR-5.

Note also that in same cases, formulae may be valid in both logics but the dialogues are different (see $\neg\neg(p\lor\neg p)$).

§14-Exercises

Case 1: D((p∧q)→p)	Case 11: D (¬¬(p∨¬p))
Case 2: D(p→(p∨q))	Case 12: D (¬¬(¬¬p→p))
Case 3: D(p∧¬p)	Case 13: D([(p∨q)∧¬p]→q)
Case 4: D((p∨q)→p)	Case 14: D([(p→q)∧p]→q)
Case 5: D((p∧q)→(q∧p))	Case 15: D[(¬p→p)→p]
Case 6: D(¬p→(p→q))	Case 16: D([(p→q)∧¬q]→¬p)
Case 7: D(p→(p∧q))	Case 17: D[((p→q)→p)→p]
Case 8: D(p∨¬p)	Case 18: D[(p→(p→q))→(p→q)]
Case 9: D(¬¬p→p)	Case 19: D[(p→s)∨(s→p)]
Case 10: D (p→¬¬p)	Case 20: D[((p→s)→(¬p→s))→s]

14.1-Game board:

a	b	c	c'	b'	a'
	O			P	
				thesis	0
1	First attack	0			

Explanations: In columns a and a' numbers that correspond to each move are placed, in columns b and b' are the moves (assertions) by O and P respectively, and in c and c' the move-target of the attacks.

14.2-Dialogue strategies: taking advantage of opponent utterances.

This may be the most important feature of the dynamic of resolution of dialogues: Given mainly to the impediment of the Proponent of asserting atomic formulae, **P** will take advantage of the answers of **O**. In fact, **P** will provoke these answers coming from **O** depending on their necessities and principally on the possibilities allowed for the rules.

Note: from here on the reader must be attentive with the use of 'to defend' and 'to respond'.

Recall that in all of the examples of the book we will assume that the Opponent has chosen rank 1 and the Proponent rank 2. In fact, in the examples displayed in the book, it is easy to verify that if the Proponent choses a higher rank than 2 the end result will not change. We leave this verification to the reader.

Case 1: $D((p \wedge q) \rightarrow p)$

(Dialogue for the thesis $(p \wedge q) \rightarrow p$)

a	B	c	c'	b'		a'
	O			P		
				$(p \wedge q) \rightarrow p$		0
1	$p \wedge q$	0		p	☺	4
3	P		1	$?\text{-}\wedge_1$		2

Explanations

Move 0: $I_1 = < \tau, \text{P-!-}(p \wedge q) \rightarrow p>$

"τ" = means that the formula is the thesis
The proponent (**P**) utters a conditional and must be defended.
Here a conditional play starts: a set of moves that concern the particle "$\rightarrow$".

Move 1: $I_2 = < \boldsymbol{CH}, \text{O-!-}(p \wedge q)> (=C_1)$

The opponent (**O**) attacks the move 0 demanding a justification for "p" conceding the left member of the conditional. The concession is a conjunction.

A new play equivalent to C_1 for X=**O** starts here. To 'start a new play' means here that attacking the conditional **O** is playing a conjunction for the first time in the dialogue and therefore beginning a new set of moves according to the rule of conjunction. It is a conjunction play: a set of moves that concern the particle "∧".

Move 2: I_3=< ***CH***, P-« attack 2 »> = < ***CH***, P-?-$\overline{\wedge_1}$> (=C_2)

P can not defend itself by responding directly "p" because it is an atomic formula and it is not yet uttered by **O**. Only **O** has the right to utter an atomic formula for the first time (SR-3).

The strategy (attack 2) consists of responding by asking for the first member: exactly what **P** needed for defending itself from the attack of move 1: "p".

The attack 2 corresponds to C_2.

Move 3: C_3=< ***D***, O-!-p>

O defends itself from the attack uttering "p".

Here the conjunction play *finished*: a set of moves that concern the particle "∧".

Move 4: I_3=< ***D***, P-!-p>

P defends itself from the attack of move 1 with the atomic formula "p" conceded by **O** in the move 3.

Here the conditional play *finished*: a set of moves that concern the particle "→".

Score
P wins by making the last move:
the dialogue is *finished* and *closed,*
O can not move further, and the same atomic
formula appears in the last two moves: 3 and 4

P has a winning strategy for the thesis!

Last remark: It is interesting to see how the series consisting of the plays of conditional and conjunction are combined strategically for the players to achieve their goals.

Moving=to perform a move

Case 2: $D(p\rightarrow(p\vee q))$

	O			P	
				$p\rightarrow(p\vee q)$	0
1	p	0		$p\vee q$	2
3	?-∨	2		p ☺	4

Move 0: $I_1=<\tau, \mathbf{P}\text{-!-}p\rightarrow(p\vee q)>$

"τ" = the formula is the thesis
P utters a conditional and must be defended.
Here *starts* a conditional play: a set of moves that concern the particle "$\rightarrow$".

Move 1: $I_2=<\mathbf{\textit{CH}}, \mathbf{O}\text{-!-}p>$

O attacks the move 0 conceding the first member of the conditional. The concession is an atomic formula ("p").

Move 2: $I_3=<\mathbf{\textit{D}}, \mathbf{P}\text{-!-}p\vee q >$

P defends itself by uttering "$p\vee q$" (because it is not an atomic formula as in the previous case).
A new play starts here that is equivalent to D_1 for X=P: a set of moves that concern the particle "$\vee$".

Move 3: $D_2=<\mathbf{\textit{CH}}, \mathbf{O}\text{-?-}\vee>$

O attacks the disjunction of move 2 according to the rule D_2.

Move 4: $D_3=<\mathbf{\textit{D}}, \mathbf{P}\text{-!-} p>$

P can defend itself from the attack of move 3 since "p" has been already uttered by **O** in the move 1. Nevertheless, he can not do the same with "q".

Score

P wins by making the last move:
the dialogue is *finished* and *closed*,
O can not move further, and the same atomic
formula appears in the moves: 1 and 4.

Case 3: $D(p \land \neg p)$

	O				P	
					$p \land \neg p$	0
1	$?-\land_1$ ☺	0				

Move 0: $C_1 = < \tau, P\text{-!-}p \land \neg p >$
Move 1: $C_2 = < \textbf{\textit{CH}}, O\text{-?-}\land_1 >$
O attacks the conjunction asking for the first member, knowing strategically that it is impossible for P to utter an atomic formula not yet utter by O. Effectively **P** can not defend itself and can not further moving according to the rules.
Score **O wins** by making the last move: the dialogue is *finished* and *open,* P can not move further, and no two positions feature the same atomic formula.

Case 4: D((p∨q)→p)

O				P	
				(p∨q)→p	0
1	p∨q	0			
			1	?-∨	2

↙   ↘

Branch 1					
O			**P**		
			(p∨q)→p	0	
1	p∨q	0			
3	q ☺	1	?-∨	2	

Branch 2					
O			**P**		
			(p∨q)→p	0	
1	p∨q	0	p ☺	4	
3	p	1	?-∨	2	

Move 0: I_1=< τ, **P**-!- (p∨q)→p >
Move 1: I_2=< **CH**, O-!-p∨q>
The opponent (**O**) attacks the move 0 conceding the first member of the conditional. The concession is a disjunction. A new play starts here that is equivalent to D_1 for X=**O**: a set of moves that concern the particle "∨".
Move 2: D_2=< **CH**, P-?-∨>
P can not defend itself by uttering directly "p" because is an atomic formula and it is not yet uttered by **O**. Instead **P** responds by attacking the disjunction of move 1. This attack 2 corresponds to D_2.
D_2 for **P** is branching time (see *Summary 3*)
Branching Time   the proponent (**P**) must win   every dialogical game that comes from the branching.

Branch 1:	Branch 2:
Move 3: D_3=< **D**, O-!-q>	Move 3: D_3=< **D**, O-!-p>

O defends itself by uttering "q".	O defends itself by uttering "p".
P is stuck	Move 4: I_3: $< D$, P-!-p$>$ **P** defends itself by uttering the atomic formula "p" conceded by **O** in the move 3.

<table>
<tr><td colspan="2" align="center">Score
O wins by making the last move (see branch 1):
the dialogue is finished and open,
P can not move further, and no two positions feature the same atomic formula.</td></tr>
</table>

Case 5: $D((p \wedge q) \rightarrow (q \wedge p))$

	O			P	
				$(p \wedge q) \rightarrow (q \wedge p)$	0
1	$p \wedge q$	0		$q \wedge p$	2

$$\swarrow \qquad \searrow$$

Branch 1

	O			P		
				$(p \wedge q) \rightarrow (q \wedge p)$		0
1	$p \wedge q$	0		$q \wedge p$		2
3	?-$\wedge_1$	2		q ☺		6
5	q		1	?-$\wedge_2$		4

Branch 2

	O			P		
				$(p \wedge q) \rightarrow (q \wedge p)$		0
1	$p \wedge q$	0		$q \wedge p$		2
3'	?-$\wedge_2$	2		p ☺		6'
5'	p		1	?-$\wedge_1$		4'

Move 0: $I_1 = < \tau$, P-!-$(p \wedge q) \rightarrow (q \wedge p) >$
Move 1: $I_2 = < CH$, O-!-$p \wedge q >$
O attacks the conditional of move 0. A new play starts here that is equivalent to C_1 for X=O: a set of moves that

concern the particle "∧".

Move 2: $I_3 = \langle D, P\text{-!-}q \wedge p \rangle$

P defends itself by uttering the second member of the conditional.
P utters "q∧p"
For the second time, a new play starts here that is equivalent to C_1 for X=P: a set of moves that concern the particle "∧".

C_1 for **P** is branching time (see *Summary 3*)

Branching Time
the proponent (**P**) must win
every dialogical game that comes from the branching.

Branch 1:	Branch 2:
Move 3: $C_2 = \langle \textit{CH}, O\text{-?-}\wedge_1 \rangle$	Move 3': $C_2 = \langle \textit{CH}, O\text{-?-}\wedge_2 \rangle$
O attacks the conjunction of move 2 by asking for the first member ("q"). The attack 2 corresponds to C_2.	**O** repeats the attack to move 2 but this time asking for the second member of the conjunction ("p").
Move 4: $C_2 = \langle \textit{CH}, P\text{-?-}\wedge_2 \rangle$	Move 4': $C_2 = \langle \textit{CH}, P\text{-?-}\wedge_1 \rangle$
P responds asking for the same element ("q") which is the second member of the conjunction uttered by **O** in move 1. Without this defence performed by **O**.	**P** responds asking for the same element ("p") which is the first member of the conjunction uttered by **O** in move 1. Without this defence performed by **O**.
Move 5: $C_3 = \langle D, O\text{-!-}q \rangle$	Move 5': $C_3 = \langle D, O\text{-!-}p \rangle$
O defends itself from the attack of move 4. **P** will not be able to perform a defence for the attack of move 3.	**O** defends itself from the attack of move 4'. **P** will not be able to perform a defence for the attack of move 3'.
Move 6: $C_3 = \langle D, P\text{-!-}q \rangle$	Move 6': $C_3 = \langle D, P\text{-!-}p \rangle$
P defends itself from the attack of	**P** defends itself from the attack of

move 3 taking advantage of the defence of move 5.	move 3' taking advantage of the defence of move 5'.

Score
P wins by making the last moves: the dialogical games are *finished* and *closed,* O can not move further, and the same atomic formula appears in the moves 5&6 and 5'&6'.

Case 6: $D(\neg p \rightarrow (p \rightarrow q))$

	O				P	
					$\neg p \rightarrow (p \rightarrow q)$	0
1	$\neg p$	0			$p \rightarrow q$	2
3	p	2				
	-		1		p ☺	4

Move 0: $I_1 = <\tau$, P-!-$(\neg p \rightarrow (p \rightarrow q))>$

Move 1: $I_2 = < CH$, O-!-$\neg p>$
O attacks the conditional of move 0. A new play starts here that is equivalent to N_1 for X=O: a set of moves that concern the particle "¬".

Move 2: $I_3 = < D$, P-!-$p \rightarrow q >$
P defends itself from the attack of move 1. A new play starts here that is equivalent to I_1 for X=**P**

Move 3: $I_2 = < CH$, O-!-p>
O attacks the conditional of move 2.

Move 4: $N_2 = < CH$, O-!-p>
Taking advantage of the atomic formula "p" uttered by O in move 3, **P** responds by attacking the negation uttered by O in move 1.

	Score
P wins by making the last move:	

Score
P wins by making the last move:
the dialogue is *finished* and *closed*,
O can not move further, and the same atomic
formula appears in the last two moves: 3 and 4.

Case 7: D(p→(p∧q))

	O			P	
				p→(p∧q)	0
1	p	0		p∧q	2
3	?-∧₂ ☺	2			

Move 0: $I_1 = <\tau,$ **P-!-p→(p∧q)>**

Move 1: $I_2 = <$ *CH*, **O-!-p>**

O attacks the conditional of move 0.

Move 2: $I_3 = <$ *D*, **P-!-p∧q >**

P defends itself by uttering the second member of the conditional.
A new play equivalent to C_1 for X=**P** starts here

Move 3: $C_2 = <$ *CH*, **O-?-∧₂>**

O attacks the conjunction of move 2 asking for the second member.

Strategically is the right choice because **P** dispose of "p" already conceded by
O but not of "q".

Score
O wins by making the last move:
the dialogue is *finished* and *open*,
P can not move further, and no two positions feature the same atomic
formula.

Case 8: D(p∨¬p) (Excluded middle)

	O				P	
					p∨¬p	0
1	?-∨	0			¬p / p ☻	2/2'
3	p	2				

Move 0: $D_1 = <\tau$, P-!-p∨¬p>

Move 1: $D_2 = < CH$, O-?-∨> O attacks the disjunction of move 0.

Move 2: $D_3 = < D$, P-!- ¬p>   P defends itself by uttering the second member of the disjunction. A new play equivalent to N_1 for X=P starts here. Note that P couldn't respond "p" because is an atomic formula not alredy uttered by O.

Move 3: $N_2 = < CH$, O-!-p>   O attacks the negation of move 2 From the intuitionistic point of view ((**RS-1** intuitionistic) + (RS-5)) the dialogue finish here and thus the thesis has not an intuitionistic winning strategy. A first **score** state: **O wins** by making the last move: the dialogue is *finished* and *open,* P can not move further, and no two positions feature the same atomic formula.

Move 2': $D_3 = < D$, P-!- p> From a classical point of view (**RS-1** classical) P can continue playing: P can repeat a defence taking advantage of the atomic formula uttered by O in move 3.

S c o r e **P wins** by making the last move: the dialogue is *finished* and *closed,* O can not move further, and the same atomic formula appears in the last two moves: 3 and 2'.

Case 9: D($\neg\neg p \rightarrow p$)

	O			P	
				$\neg\neg p \rightarrow p$	0
1	$\neg\neg p$	0		p ☻	4
	-		1	$\neg p$	2
3	p	2		-	

Move 0: $I_1 = <\tau$, P-!-$\neg\neg p \rightarrow p$>

Move 1: $I_2 = < CH,$ O-!-$\neg\neg p$>

O attacks the conditional of move 0.
A new play starts here that is equivalent to N_1 for X=**O**: a set of moves that concern the particle "$\neg$".

Move 2: $N_2 = < CH,$ P-!-$\neg p$>

P responds by attacking the negation of move 1.
A new play equivalent to N_1 for X=**P** starts here

Move 3: $N_2 = < CH,$ O-!-p>

Since there is no possible defence for a negation, then **O** responds by attacking the negation of move 2.

From an intuitionistic point of view (($\textbf{RS-1}$ $_{\text{intuitionistic}}$) + (RS-5)) the dialogue finish here and thus the thesis has not a winning strategy.

A first **score** state:
O wins by making the last move:
the dialogue is *finished* and *open,*
P can not move further, and no two positions feature the same atomic formula

Move 4: $I_3 = < D,$ P-!-p>

From classical point of view **P** can continue playing: taking advantage of the atomic formula uttered by **O** in move 3, **P** defends itself from the attack made by **O** in move 1. Note that it is not the last attack, but with classical rules (**RS-**

$1_{\text{classical}}$) is allowed.

Score
P wins by making the last move:
the dialogue is *finished* and *closed*,
O can not move further, and the same atomic
formula appears in the last two moves: 3 and 4.

Resume: there is not an intuitionistic winning strategy for the thesis but a classical one.

Case 10: $D(p \rightarrow \neg\neg p)$

	O				P	
					$p \rightarrow \neg\neg p$	0
1	p	0			$\neg\neg p$	2
3	$\neg p$	2			-	
	-			3	p ☺	4

Move 0: $I_1 = <\tau\,,\ \mathbf{P}\text{-!-}p \rightarrow \neg\neg p>$
Move 1: $I_2 = <\mathbf{CH},\ \mathbf{O}\text{-!-}p>$
Move 2: $I_3 = <\mathbf{D},\ \mathbf{P}\text{-!-}\neg\neg p>$
A new play equivalent to N_1 for X= **P** starts here
Move 3: $N_2 = <\mathbf{CH},\ \mathbf{O}\text{-!-}\neg p>$
A new play equivalent to N_1 for X= **O** starts here
Move 4: $N_2 = <\mathbf{CH},\ \mathbf{P}\text{-!-}p>$
P takes advantage of the atomic formula uttered by **O** in move 1 and attacks the negation asserted by **O** in move 3
Score
P wins by making the last move:
the dialogue is *finished* and *closed*,
O can not move further, and the same atomic
formula appears in the moves: 1 and 4.

Case 11: $D(\neg\neg(p \vee \neg p))$

	O			P	
				$\neg\neg(p \vee \neg p)$	0
1	$\neg(p \vee \neg p)$	0		-	
	-		1	$p \vee \neg p$	2
3	?-∨	2		$\neg p$	4
5	p	4		-	
			1	$p \vee \neg p$	6
7	?-∨	6		p ☺	8

Move 0: $N_1 = <\tau, P\text{-!-}\neg\neg(p \vee \neg p))>$
Move 1: $N_2 = < \textbf{\textit{CH}}, O\text{-!-}\neg(p \vee \neg p)$ A new play equivalent to N_1 for X= **O** starts here
Move 2: $N_2 = < \textbf{\textit{CH}}, P\text{-!-}(p \vee \neg p)>$ A new play equivalent to D_1 for X= **P** starts here
Move 3: $D_2 = < \textbf{\textit{CH}}, O\text{-?-}\vee>$ **O** attacks the disjunction of move 2
Move 4: $D_3 = < \textbf{\textit{D}}, P\text{-!-}\neg p>$ **P** defend itself by uttering "¬p" A new play starts here equivalent to N_1 for X= **P** Note that **P** couldn't answer uttering "p" but only "¬p" in this move
Move 5: $N_2 = < \textbf{\textit{CH}}, O\text{-!-}p>$ **O** attacks the negation of move 4
Move 6: $N_2 = < \textbf{\textit{CH}}, P\text{-!-}(p \vee \neg p)>$ **P** responds by attacking again the negation of move 1. Note that this move is allowed with classical rules since a new information has been uttered by **O** in move 5 (see **SR-5**)
Move 7: $D_2 = < \textbf{\textit{CH}}, O\text{-?-}\vee>$

O attacks the disjunction of move 6
Move 8: $D_3 = < D$, P-!-p>
Taking advantage of the information uttered by O in move 5, P defends itself uttering "p".
Score **P wins** by making the last move: the dialogue is *finished* and *closed,* O can not move further, and the same atomic formula appears in the moves: 5 and 8.

Note: the dialogue above correspond to an *intuitionistic winning strategy* for the thesis – take into consideration that even if **P** chooses rank 2, he can not defend twice because of the intuitionistic rule. If a formula has an intuitionistic winning strategy, thus it has a winning strategy in classical logic. But in this case the corresponding dialogue is different. Indeed, in move 6 we used the rule (RS-5) which allows **P** to repeat an attack (since we assumed through all the book that P has chosen the rank 2). However, in classical logic the P has a simpler option. In fact, to get a winning strategy according to classical logic, it suffices that **P** reiterates his defence of move 4 (opting for the same strategy as in the case of Excluded Middle: see case 8)

	O			**P**	
				¬¬(p∨¬p)	0
1	¬(p∨¬p)	0		-	
	-		1	(p∨¬p)	2
3	?-∨	2		¬p/p ☺	4/4'
5	p	4		-	

Move 0: $N_1 = <\tau$, P-!-¬¬(p∨¬p)>
Move 1: $N_2 = < CH$, O-!-¬(p∨¬p)>
Move 2: $N_2 = < CH$, P-!-(p∨¬p)>
Move 3: $D_2 = < CH$, O-?-∨>
Move 4: $D_3 = < D$, P-!-¬p>
Move 5: $N_2 = < CH$, O-!-p>

Move 4': D₃= < D, P-!-p>
See Case 8

Score
P **wins** by making the last move:
the dialogue is *finished* and *closed*,
O can not move further, and the same atomic
formula appears in the last two moves: 4' and 5.

Case 12: D(¬¬(¬¬p→p))

	O				P	
					¬¬(¬¬p→p)	0
1	¬(¬¬p→p)	0			-	
			1		¬¬p→p	2
3	¬¬p	2				
			3		¬p	4
5	p	4			-	
			1		¬¬p→p	6
7	¬¬p	6			p ☺	8

Move 0: N₁= <τ , P-!-¬¬(¬¬p→p)>
Move 1: N₂= < CH, O-!-¬(¬¬p→p)>
Move 2: N₂= < CH, P-!-(¬¬p→p)>
Move 3: I₂= < CH, O-!-¬¬p>
Move 4: N₂= < CH, P-!-¬p>
Move 5: N₂= < CH, O-!-p>
Move 6: N₂= < CH, P-!-(¬¬p →p)>
Move 7: I₂=< CH, O-!-¬¬p>
Move 8: I₃=< D, P-!-p>
P takes advantage of the utterance of move 5.
Score

> **P wins** by making the last move:
> the dialogue is *finished* and *closed,*
> O can not move further, and the same atomic
> formula appears in the moves: 5 and 8.

Note: as in case 11, the dialogue above corresponds to an *intuitionistic winning strategy* for the thesis. For a classical winning strategy see below.

	O				P	
					$\neg\neg(\neg\neg p \rightarrow p)$	0
1	$\neg(\neg\neg p \rightarrow p)$	0			-	
	-		1		$\neg\neg p \rightarrow p$	2
3	$\neg\neg p$	2			p ☻	6
	-		3		$\neg p$	4
5	p	4			-	

Move 0: $N_1 = <- , P\text{-!-}\neg\neg(\neg\neg p \rightarrow p)$
Move 1: $N_2 = < \textit{CH}, O\text{-!-}\neg(\neg\neg p \rightarrow p)$
Move 2: $N_2 = < \textit{CH}, P\text{-!-}(\neg\neg p \rightarrow p)>$
Move 3: $I_2 = < \textit{CH}, O\text{-!-}\neg\neg p>$
Move 4: $N_2 = < \textit{CH}, P\text{-!-}\neg p >$
Move 5: $N_2 = < \textit{CH}, O\text{-!-}p>$
Move 6: $N_2 = < \textit{D}, P\text{-!-}p>$
Note that this defence is not allowed in intuitionistic logic
Score
P wins by making the last move:
the dialogue is *finished* and *closed,*
O can not move further, and the same atomic
formula appears in the last two moves: 5 and 6.

Case 13: $D([(p\lor q)\land\neg p]\to q)$

O				P	
				$[(p\lor q)\land\neg p]\to q$	0
1	$[(p\lor q)\land\neg p]$	0			
3	$\neg p$		1	?-$\land_2$	2
5	$p\lor q$		1	?-$\land_1$	4
			5	?-$\lor$	6

↙ ↘

Branch 1

O				P	
				$[(p\lor q)\land\neg p]\to q$	0
1	$[(p\lor q)\land\neg p]$	0			
3	$\neg p$		1	?-$\land_2$	2
5	$p\lor q$		1	?-$\land_1$	4
7	p		5	?-$\lor$	6
			3	p ☺	8

Branch 2

O				P	
				$[(p\lor q)\land\neg p]\to q$	0
1	$[(p\lor q)\land\neg p]$	0		q ☺	8'
3	$\neg p$		1	?-$\land_2$	2
5	$p\lor q$		1	?-$\land_1$	4
7'	q		5	?-$\lor$	6

Move 0: I_1=<- , P-!-$([(p\lor q)\land\neg p]\to q)$>
Move 1: I_2=< **CH**, O- !-$([(p\lor q)\land\neg p])$>
Move 2: C_2=< **CH**, P-?-$\land_2$>
Move 3: C_3=< **D**, O-!- $\neg p$>
Move 4: C_2=< **CH**, P-?-$\land_1$>
Move 5: C_3=< **D**, O-!-$p\lor q$>
Move 6: D_2=< **CH**, P-?-$\lor$>

Branching Time
[Def. 6, (i)]
the proponent (P) must win both dialogical games.

BRANCH 1	BRANCH 2
Move 7: D_3=< **D**, O-!-p>	Move 7: D_3=< **D**, O-!-q>
Move 8: N_2=< **CH**, P-!-p> ☺	Move 8: I_3=< **D**, P-!-q> ☺

Score

> **P wins** by making the last moves:
> the dialogical games are *finished* and *closed*,
> O can not move further, and the same atomic
> formula appears in the moves 7&8 and 7'&8'.

Case 14: $D([(p{\rightarrow}q){\wedge}p]{\rightarrow}q)$

	O			P	
				$[(p{\rightarrow}q){\wedge}p]{\rightarrow}q$	0
1	$(p{\rightarrow}q){\wedge}p$	0			
3	p	1		?-${\wedge}_2$	2
5	$p{\rightarrow}q$	1		?-${\wedge}_1$	4
			5	p	6

↙   ↘

Branch 1	Branch 2

	O			P	
				$[(p{\rightarrow}q){\wedge}p]{\rightarrow}q$	0
1	$(p{\rightarrow}q){\wedge}p$	0		q ☺	8
3	p	1		?-${\wedge}_2$	2
5	$p{\rightarrow}q$	1		?-${\wedge}_1$	4
7	q		5	p	6

	O			P	
				$[(p{\rightarrow}q){\wedge}p]{\rightarrow}q$	0
1	$(p{\rightarrow}q){\wedge}p$	0			
3	p	1		?-${\wedge}_2$	2
5	$p{\rightarrow}q$	1		?-${\wedge}_1$	4
			5	p	6

Move 0: I_1=<- , **P**-!-$[(p{\rightarrow}q){\wedge}p]{\rightarrow}q$>
Move 1: I_2=< **CH**, O-!-$[(p{\rightarrow}q){\wedge}p]$>
Move 2: C_2=< **CH**, P-?-${\wedge}_2$>
Move 3: C_3=< **D**, O-!-p>
Move 4: C_2=< **CH**, P-?-${\wedge}_1$>
Move 5: C_3=< **D**, O-!-p{\rightarrow}q>
Move 6: I_2=< **CH**, P-!-p>
Branching time   [Def. 6, (iii)]   P must win both dialogical games.

BRANCH 1	BRANCH 2

Move 7: $I_3 = <D, O\text{-!-}q>$	Null because O cannot attacks an atomic formula.
Move 8: $I_3 = <D, P\text{-!-}q>$ ☺	

Score
P wins by making the last moves:
the dialogical games are *finished* and *closed*,
O can not move further, and the same atomic
formula appears in the moves 7&8 and 3&6.

Case 15: $D[(\neg p \rightarrow p) \rightarrow p]$

	O				P	
					$(\neg p \rightarrow p) \rightarrow p$	0
1	$\neg p \rightarrow p$	0				
			1		$\neg p$	2

↙ ↘

Branch 1

	O				P	
					$(\neg p \rightarrow p) \rightarrow p$	0
1	$\neg p \rightarrow p$	0				
			1		$\neg p$	2
3	p ☺	2			-	

Branch 2

	O				P	
					$(\neg p \rightarrow p) \rightarrow p$	0
1	$\neg p \rightarrow p$	0			p ☺	4'
3'	p		1		$\neg p$	2

Move 0: $I_1 = <\tau, P\text{-!-}(\neg p \rightarrow p) \rightarrow p>$	
Move 1: $I_2 = <CH, O\text{-!-}(\neg p \rightarrow p)>$	
Move 2: $I_2 = <CH, P\text{- !- } \neg p>$	

Branching time
[Def. 6, (iii)]
P must win both dialogical games.

BRANCH 1	**BRANCH 2**
Move 3: $N_2 = <CH, O\text{-!-}p>$	Move 3': $I_3 = <D, O\text{-!-}p>$
	Move 4': $I_3 = <D, P\text{-!-}p>$

A first **S c o r e** state:
O wins by making the last move:
the dialogue is *finished* and *open,*
P can not move further, and no two positions feature the same atomic
formula.
The thesis has not an intuitionistic winning strategy

We continue playing with classical rules:

	O				P	
					$(\neg p \rightarrow p) \rightarrow p$	0
1	$\neg p \rightarrow p$	0				
				1	$\neg p$	2

Branch **1**

	O				P	
					$(\neg p \rightarrow p) \rightarrow p$	0
1	$\neg p \rightarrow p$	0			p ☻	4
				1	$\neg p$	2
3	p	2			-	

Branch **2**

	O				P	
					$(\neg p \rightarrow p) \rightarrow p$	0
1	$\neg p \rightarrow p$	0			p ☻	4'
3'	p		1		$\neg p$	2

Remember ☻ = valid only in classical logic

Move 0: $I_1 = <\tau , \text{P-!-}(\neg p \rightarrow p) \rightarrow p>$	
Move 1: $I_2 = < \textbf{\textit{CH}}, \text{O-!-}(\neg p \rightarrow p)>$	
Move 2: $I_2 = < \textbf{\textit{CH}}, \text{P- !- } \neg p>$	
Branching time [Def. 6, (iii)] P must win both dialogical games.	
BRANCH 1	**BRANCH 2**
Move 3: $N_2 - < \textbf{\textit{CH}}, \text{O ! p}>$	Move 3': $I_3 - < \textbf{\textit{D}}, \text{O-!-p}>$
Move 4: $I_3 = < \textbf{\textit{D}}, \text{P-!-p}>$ P defends itself from the attack to move 1 which is not the last attack, therefore the thesis is valid only in classical logic.	Move 4': $I_3 = < \textbf{\textit{D}}, \text{P-!-p}>$

> ### Score
> **P wins** by making the last moves:
> the dialogical games are *finished* and *closed,*
> **O** can not move further, and the same atomic
> formula appears in the moves 3&4 and 3'&4'.

Case 16: $D([(p{\rightarrow}q)\wedge\neg q]{\rightarrow}p)$

	O			P	
				$[(p{\rightarrow}q) \wedge\neg q]{\rightarrow} \neg p$	0
1	$[(p{\rightarrow}q) \wedge\neg q]$	0		$\neg p$	2
3	p	2		-	
5	$\neg q$		1	$?\text{-}\wedge_2$	4
7	$p{\rightarrow}q$		1	$?\text{-}\wedge_1$	6
9	q		7	p	8
	-		5	q ☺	10

Note that we did the dialogue only with Branch 1

Move 0: I_1=<- , P-!-$[(p{\rightarrow}q)\wedge\neg q]{\rightarrow}\neg p$>
Move 1: I_2=< **CH**, O-!-$[(p{\rightarrow}q) \wedge\neg q]$>
Move 2: I_3=< **D**, P-!-$\neg p$>
Move 3: N_2=< **CH**, O-!-p>
Move 4: C_2=< **CH**, P-?-$\wedge_2$>
Move 5: C_3=< **D**, O-!-$\neg q$ >
Move 6: C_2=< **CH**, P-?-$\wedge_1$>
Move 7: C_3=< **D**, O-!-p$\rightarrow$q>
Move 8: I_2=< **CH**, P-!-p>

Branching time
[Def. 6, (*iii*)]
P must win both dialogical games.

BRANCH 1	BRANCH 2
Move 9: I_3=< **D**, O-!-q>	Null because O cannot attacks an

Move 10: N_2=< **CH**, P-!-q> ☺	atomic formula.

Score
P wins by making the last moves:
the dialogical games are *finished* and *closed*,
O can not move further, and the same atomic
formula appears in the moves 9 and 10.

Case 17: D[((p→q)→p)→p] (Law of Peirce)

	O				P	
					((p→q)→p)→p	0
1	((p→q)→p)	0				
				1	(p→q)	2

↙ ↘

Branch 1

	O				P	
					((p→q)→p)→p	0
1	((p→q)→p)	0			p ●	4
				1	(p→q)	2
3	p ☺	2				

Branch 2

	O				P	
					((p→q)→p)→p	0
1	((p→q)→p)	0			p ● ☺	4
3	p		1	(p→q)	2

Move 0: I_1=<- , P-!-((p→q)→p)→p >
Move 1: I_2=< **CH**, O-!-((p→q)→p)>
Move 2: I_2=< **D**, P-!- (p→q)>

Branching time
[Def. 6, (iii)]
P must win both dialogical games.

BRANCH 1	BRANCH 2
Move 3: I_2=< **CH**, O-!-p> With intuitionistic rules the dialogical game <u>stops</u> here.	Move 3: I_3=< **D**, O-!-p>
Move 4: I_3=< **D**, P- !-p> ●	Move 4: I_3=< **D**, P- !-p> ● ☺

First **Score**[☺]:

> **O wins** by making the last move:
> the dialogue is *finished* and *open*,
> **P** can not move further, and no two positions feature the same atomic
> formula.
> The thesis has not an intuitionistic winning strategy.
>
> Second **S c o r e** [●]:
> **P wins** by making the last move:
> the dialogical games are *finished* and *closed*,
> **O** can not move further, and the same atomic
> formula appears in the moves 3 and 4 in both branches.
>
> The thesis has a classical winning strategy.

Case 18: D[(p→(p→q))→(p→q)]

	O			P	
				(p→(p→q))→(p→q)	0
1	p→(p→q)	0		(p→q)	2
3	p	2		q☺	8
5	p→q		1	p	4
7	q		5	p	6

Move 0: I_1=<τ , **P**-!-(p→(p→q))→(p→q)>
Move 1: I_2=< **CH**, O-!-(p→(p→q))>
Move 2: I_3=< **D**, P-!-(p→q)>
Move 3: I_2=< **CH**, O-!-p>
Move 4: I_2=< **CH**, P-!-p>
Here corresponds to make a branching, but one of them is null (see cases 14 a nd 16)
Move 5: I_3=< **D**, O-!-p→q>
Move 6: I_2=< **CH**, P-!-p>

Here corresponds to make a branching, but one of them is null (see cases 14 a nd 16)
Move 7: I_3=< D, O-!- q>
Move 8: I_3=< D, P-!- q>
Score   **P wins** by making the last move: the dialogue is *finished* and *closed*,   O can not move further, and the same atomic   formula appears in the moves: 7 and 8.

Case 19: $D[(p{\rightarrow}s)\vee(s{\rightarrow}p)]$

	O				P	
					$(p{\rightarrow}s)\vee(s{\rightarrow}p)$	0
1	?-∨	0			$p{\rightarrow}s$	2
3	p	2			s ●	6
					$s{\rightarrow}p$	4
5	s ☺	4				

Move 0: D_1=<τ, **P**-!-$(p{\rightarrow}s)\vee(s{\rightarrow}p)$>
Move 1: D_2=< *CH*, O-?-∨>
Move 2: D_3=< D, P-!-$(p{\rightarrow}s)$>
Move 3: I_2=< *CH*, O-!-p>
Move 4: D_3=< D, P-!-$(s{\rightarrow}p)$>   P reiterates his defence of move 1
Move 5: I_2=< *CH*, O-!-s>   With intuitionistic rules the dialogical game stops here.
Move 6: I_3=< D, P-!-s>
First **Score**[☺]:   **O wins** by making the last move:

the dialogue is *finished* and *open*,
P can not move further, and no two positions feature the same atomic formula
The thesis has not an intuitionistic winning strategy.

Second **Score** [●]:
P wins by making the last move:
the dialogue is *finished* and *closed*,
O can not move further, and the same atomic formula appears in the moves 5 and 6 in both branches.

The thesis has a classical winning strategy.

Case 20: D[((p→s)∧(¬p→s))→ s]

	O				P	
					((p→s)∧(¬p→s))→s	0
1	(p→s)∧(¬p→s)	0				
3	¬p→s	1		?-∧₂		2
			3	¬p		4

↙ ↘

Branch 1

	O				P	
					((p→s)∧(¬p→s))→s	0
1	(p→s)∧(¬p→s)	0		s ●		10
3	¬p→s	1		?-∧₂		2
			3	¬p		4
5	p	4				
7	p→s	1		?-∧₁		6
9	s ☺		7	p		8

Branch 2

	O				P	
					((p→s)∧(¬p→s))→s	0
1	(p→s)∧(¬p→s)	0		s ● ☺		6
3	¬p→s	1		?-∧₂		2
5	s		3	¬p		4

Move 0: $I_1 = <\text{-}, \text{P-!-}((p \to s) \land (\neg p \to s)) \to s>$
Move 1: $I_2 = <\textbf{\textit{CH}}, \text{O-}((p \to s) \land (\neg p \to s))>$
Move 2: $C_2 = <\textbf{\textit{CH}}, \text{P-?-}\land_2>$
Move 3: $C_3 = <\textbf{\textit{D}}, \text{O-!-}\neg p \to s>$
Move 4: $I_2 = <\textbf{\textit{CH}}, \text{P-!-}\neg p>$

Branching time
[Def. 6, (iii)]
The proponent (**P**) must win both dialogical games.

BRANCH 1	BRANCH 2
Move 5: $N_2 = <\textbf{\textit{CH}}, \text{O-!-}p>$	Move 5: $I_3 = <\textbf{\textit{D}}, \text{O-!-}s>$
Move 6: $C_2 = <\textbf{\textit{CH}}, \text{P-?-}\land_1>$	Move 6: $I_3 = <\textbf{\textit{D}}, \text{P-!-}s>$
Move 7: $C_3 = <\textbf{\textit{D}}, \text{O-!-}p \to s>$	
Move 8: $I_2 = <\textbf{\textit{CH}}, \text{P-!-}p>$	
Move 9: $I_3 = <\textbf{\textit{D}}, \text{O-!-}s>$	
Move 10: $I_3 = <\textbf{\textit{D}}, \text{P-!-}s>$	

First **S c o r e** [☺]:
O wins by making the last move:
the dialogue is *finished* and *open*,
P can not move further, and no two positions feature the same atomic
formula.
The thesis has not an intuitionistic winning strategy.

Second **S c o r e** [☻]:
P wins by making the last move:
the dialogue is *finished* and *closed*,
O can not move further, and the same atomic
formula appears in the moves 9&10 and 5&6.

FIRST ORDER DIALOGICAL LOGIC

§15. Language for first order logic (FOL)

A vocabulary **L** for first order logic consists of a set of individual constants k_1, k_2, ... (k_i); a set of relational symbols P, Q, ... (predicate constants of degree n); a set of individual variables x, y, ...; the symbols "$\forall$" and "$\exists$" called respectively universal and existential quantifiers; the same connectives of propositional logic: negation "$\neg$", conjunction "$\wedge$", disjunction "$\vee$", conditional "$\rightarrow$", and the brackets ")"and "(".

The well-formed formulas of first order logic are expressions inductively defined as follows:

(1) Each propositional letter is, on its own, a wff.
(2) If φ is a wff, then $\neg\varphi$ is a wff.
(3) If φ and θ are wffs, and "&" is a binary connective, then "$\varphi\&\theta$" is a wff. Here "&" could be "$\vee$", "$\wedge$" or "$\rightarrow$".
(4) If φ is a wff, then $\forall x\varphi$ and $\exists x\varphi$ are wff.
(5) Only what can be generated by clauses (1) to (3) in a finite number of steps is a wff.

§16. Language for first order dialogical logic (FOdL)

We define the language for first order dialogical logic as the result of enriching the language of first order logic (**FOL**) with the following metalogical symbols:

two force symbols **?** and **!**;
the symbols 1, 2; $\forall/k_i$, $\exists$ (k_i is any constant)
two labels **O** and **P** (standing for the players, Opponent and Proponent, respectively).

§17. Particle Rules

Universal quantifier

$\forall$		
Formula uttered	Attack	Defence
$\forall x \varphi$	A question	A formula
dialogical expressions:		
X-!-$\forall x \varphi$	Y-?-k_i	X-!-$\varphi[x/k_i]^{13}$

Explanation 1

X utters a universal quantified formula ($\forall x \varphi$) that must be defended (!). Upon uttering $\forall x \varphi$, the player **X** commits himself to uttering $\varphi[x/k_i]$ for any k_i. How does **Y** challenge the utterance "$\forall x \varphi$"? By demanding the utterance of $\varphi[x/k_i]$. However, since **X** commits itself to the utterance of $\varphi[x/k_i]$ for any k_i, the challenger **Y** has the right to decide for which one the player **X** should perform the utterance (Y-?-k_i). The defence consists of uttering $\varphi[x/k_i]$, when possible, for the k_i chosen by **Y**.[14]

Existential quantifier

$\exists$		
Formula uttered	Attack	Defence
$\exists x \varphi$	A question	A formula
dialogical expressions:		
X-!-$\exists x \varphi$	Y-?	X-!-$\varphi[x/k_i]$

Explanation 2

X utters an existential quantified formula ($\exists x \varphi$) that must be defended (!). Upon uttering $\exists x \varphi$, the player **X** commits himself to uttering $\varphi[x/k_i]$ for <u>at least</u> one k_i. How does **Y** challenge the utterance $\exists x \varphi$? By demanding the utterance of

---

[13] For example: $\varphi[x]$= "x is an Argentine", k_i = an individual (any), for example: Juan; So $\varphi[x/k_i]$= "Juan is an Argentine"

[14] For example: when the Captain of a cargo ship transporting boxes says to the customs officer (who is performing some control over the carried boxes), that every box has apples ($\forall x \varphi$), it is not the Captain who will choose the boxes the officer will check out if the Captain told the truth.

$\varphi[x/k_i]$. However, since **X** commits himself to the utterance of $\varphi[x/k_i]$ <u>for at least</u> one k_i, **X** has the right to decide which one. The defence consists of uttering $\varphi[x/k_i]$, when possible, for the k_i chosen by **X** (X-!-$\varphi[x/k_i]$).

Summary 4

		Assertion	Attaque	Défense
i	∧	**X**-!-A∧B	Y-?-∧₁ Y-?-∧₂	**X**-!-A **X**-!-B
ii	∨	**X**-!-A∨B	Y-?-∨	**X**-!-A ou **X**-!-B
iii	→	**X**-!-A→B	Y-!-A	**X**-!-B
iv	¬	**X**-!-¬A	Y-!-A	Il n'y a pas
v	∀	**X**-!- ∀xφ	Y-?- x/k_i **Y** has the choice	**X**-!-$\varphi[x/k_i]$
vi	∃	**X**-!-∃xφ	Y-?-∃x	**X**-!-$\varphi[x/k_i]$ **X** has the choice

§18. States of dialogue for every particle

Particle rule for the universal quantifier (U)

The play begins with a universally quantified formula: $\Psi = \forall x\varphi$.

Players	dialogical expressions	Explanations
X	Move U₁= <--, X-!- ∀xφ >	**X** utters the formula ∀xφ and must defend it (!)
Y	Move U₂= < *CH,* Y-?-k_i >	**Y** attacks (*CH*) asking (?) for a k_i of his choice.
X	Move U₃= < *D,* X-!-$\varphi[x/k_i]$>	**X** defends itself performing the utterance required.

Particle rule for the existential quantifier (E)

The play begins with an existentially quantified formula: $\Psi = \exists x\varphi$.

Players	dialogical expressions	Explanations
X	Move $E_1 = <\text{--}, X\text{-!-}\exists x\varphi >$	**X** utters the formula $\exists x\varphi$ and must defend it (!)
Y	Move $E_2 = < CH, Y\text{-?-}\exists >$	**Y** attacks (***CH***) asking (?) for at least one k_i.
X	Move $E_3 = < D, X\text{-!-}\varphi[x/k_i] >$	**X** defends itself choosing a k_i and performing the utterance required.

§19. Dialogues in action: an illustration

❧ Illustration for the universal quantifier ❧

If X=P

	O			P	
				$\forall x\varphi$	U_1
U_2	?- k_i			$\varphi[x/k_i]$	U_3

	Details
$U_1=$	$< \text{--}, P\text{-!-}\forall x\varphi>$
$U_2=$	$< CH, O\text{-?-}k_i >$
$U_3=$	$< D, P\text{-!-}\varphi[x/k_i]>$

If X=O

	O			P	
U_1	$\forall x\varphi$				
U_3	$\varphi[x/k_i]$			?- k_i	U_2

	Details
$U_1=$	$< \text{--}, O\text{-!-}\forall x\varphi>$
$U_2=$	$< CH, P\text{-?-} k_i >$
$U_3=$	$< D, O\text{-!-}\varphi[x/k_i]>$

❧ Illustration for the existential quantifier ❧

If X=P

	O			P	
				$\exists x\varphi$	E_1
E_2	?-$\exists$			$\varphi[x/k_i]$	E_3

	Details
$E_1=$	$< \text{--}, P\text{-!-}\exists x\varphi >$
$E_2=$	$< CH, O\text{-?-}\exists >$
$E_3=$	$< D, P\text{-!-}\varphi[x/k_i]>$

If X = O

	O			P			Details	
						$E_1=$	$< --, P\text{-!-} x\varphi>$	
E_1	$x\varphi$					$E_2=$	$< CH, P\text{-?-} >$	
E_3	$\varphi\,[x/k_i]$			?-	E_2	$E_3=$	$< D, O\text{-!-}\varphi\,[x/k_i]>$	

Summary 5

State of dialogue=$<\rho, \Phi>$

$\Phi = P\text{-!-}\Psi,\ O\text{-!-}\Psi,\ P\text{-?-}\text{Ж et } O\text{-?-}\text{Ж}$

Ψ for the first move: $\neg A,\ A \wedge B,\ A \vee B,\ A \rightarrow B,\ \exists x\varphi,\ \forall x\varphi$

Ψ for the second move corresponding to N2, C2, etc.

Ж is the target of a question and is always an attack.

expressions	In the same order:
$< CH, Y\text{-?-}\text{Ж} >$	\<attack, player Y-question-target>
$< CH, Y\text{-!-}A>$	< attack, player Y-to defend-formule-A>
$< D, X\text{-!-}B>$	< defence, player X- to defend-formule -B>

§20. Structural rules

(SR-0) (*Start*): The expressions of a dialogue are numbered, and are alternately asserted by **P** and **O**. The *thesis* carries the number 0, and is asserted by **P**. All moves after the thesis obey particle and structural rules. We will call D(A) a dialogue D that starts with the thesis A. The even moves (2, 4, ...) are moves made by **P**, the odd moves (1, 3, ...) are made by **O**.

(SR-1 intuitionistic) (*Intuitionistic round closing rule*)
Every time, every player can either attack a complex formula uttered by the other player or defend itself from the *last undefended attack* (the *last* attack against which the player still is not defended). If it is the turn of X to perform the move n, and Y has already performed two attacks in the moves *l* and *m*

($l<m<n$) that X has not defended yet, X cannot defend itself any more against l. In brief, the only possible defence is against the last undefended attack.

(SR-1 classical) (*Classical round closing rule*)

Every time, every player can either attack a complex formula uttered by the other player or defend itself from *any undefended attack* (including those which have already been defended).

(SR-2) (*Branching*)

If in a play it is **O**'s turn to make the choice to either defend a disjunction, attack a conjunction, or react to an attack against a conditional, **O** produces two separate dialogues: a branching devides a dialogue into two *dialogical games*. **O** switches from one dialogical game to the other if and only if **O** loses the first one.

(SR-3) (*Formal use of atomic formulae*)

Atomic formulas (formulas without connectors or particules) can be uttered *for the first time* only by **O**. The proponent (**P**) can play an atomic formula only if the same formula was already uttered by **O**. Atomic formulae cannot be attacked.

(SR-4) (*Winning rule for plays*)

A dialogue is *closed* if and only if there appears the same atomic formula in two subsequent positions, one uttered by X and the other by Y. Otherwise the dialogue is still *open*.

The player who utters the thesis *wins* if and only if the dialogue is closed. A dialogue is *finished* if and only if it is closed or there is no further move to do according to the rules (of particles and structurals). The opponent wins if and only if the dialogue is finished and open.

To introduce the next rule we define the concept of *repetition*:

(SR-5) (*No delaying tactics rule*)

The same rule as before:

After the move that sets the thesis, and befote starting the gameplayers O and P each choose a natural number n and m respectively (termed their repetition ranks). Thereafter the players move alternately, each move being a request or an answer.

In the course of the dialogue, O (P) may attack or defend any single (token of an) utterance at most n (or m) times and in agreement with SR-1.[15]

Also in the first-order- case we will assume that the Opponent has chosen rank 1 and the Proponent rank 2.

(**Definition 10**) [*Winning strategy*]
The thesis A has a *dialogically winning strategy* in the classical or intuitionistic sense, if and only if all games belonging to the respective dialogue are closed.

---

[15] Nicolas Clerbout [2011] proved soundness and completeness of dialogues for first-order logic for a dialogical framework that makes use of the notion of ranks.

§21. Exercises

Case 21: D($\forall x\phi \rightarrow \forall x\phi$)

	O				P	
					$\forall x\phi \rightarrow \forall x\phi$	0
1	$\forall x\phi$	0			$\forall x\phi$	2
3	?-ki	2			$\phi[x/\text{ki}]$ ☺	6
5	$\phi[x/\text{ki}]$		1		?- ki	4

Move 0: $I_1 = <\tau, P\text{-!-}\forall x\phi \rightarrow \forall x\phi >$

The proponent (**P**) utters a conditional and must defend it.
A conditional play starts here: a set of moves that concern the particle "$\rightarrow$".

Move 1: $I_2 = < CH, O\text{-!-}\forall x\phi>$

The opponent (**O**) attacks the conditional conceding the first member.
A new play equivalent to U_1 for X=**O** starts here: a set
of moves that concern "$\forall$".

Move 2: $I_3 = < D, P\text{-!-}\forall x\phi>$

P defends itself uttering the second member.
A new play equivalent to U_1 for X= **P** starts here: a set
of moves that concern "$\forall$".

Move 3: $U_2 = < CH, O\text{-?-ki} >$

O attacks the universal quantifier by asking for the constant ki.

Move 4: $U_2 = < CH, P\text{-?-ki} >$

P made the same attack for taking advantage of the utterance of **O**.
Note that in moves 1 and 2 the utterances are identical.

Move 5: $U_3 = < D, O\text{-!-}\phi[x/\text{ki}]>$

O defends itself uttering that ϕ stands for ki.

Move 6: $U_3 = < D, P\text{-!-}\phi[x/\text{ki}]>$ ☺

Taking advantage of the precedent utterance, **P** defends itself.
Score **P wins** by making the last move: the dialogue is *finished* and *closed,* **O** can not move further, and the same atomic formula appears in the last two moves: 5&6.

Below we show two specific cases, when $\phi = Px \rightarrow Qx$, and when $\phi = Px \wedge Qx$.

1) $\phi = Px \rightarrow Qx$

	O				P	
				$\forall x(Px \rightarrow Qx) \rightarrow \forall x\,(Px \rightarrow Qx)$		0
1	$\forall x(Px \rightarrow Qx)$	0			$\forall x(Px \rightarrow Qx)$	2
3	?-ki	2			$Pki \rightarrow Qki$	4
5	Pki	4			Qki ☺	10
7	$Pki \rightarrow Qki$	1			?-ki	6
9	Qki	7			Pki	8

Move 0: $I_1 = <\tau\,, \textbf{P-!-}\forall x(Px \rightarrow Qx) \rightarrow \forall x\,(Px \rightarrow Qx)>$
Move 1: $I_2 = <\textbf{\textit{CH}}, \textbf{O-!-}\forall x(Px \rightarrow Qx)>$ **O** attacks the conditional of move 0. A new play equivalent to U_1 for X=**O** starts here
Move 2: $I_3 = <\textbf{\textit{D}}, \textbf{P-!-}\forall x(Px \rightarrow Qx)>$ **P** defends itself by uttering the second member of the conditional. A new play equivalent to U_1 for X=**P** starts here
Move 3: $U_2 = <\textbf{\textit{CH}}, \textbf{O-?-ki}>$ **O** attacks the universal quantifier by asking for the constant ki
Move 4: $U_3 = <\textbf{\textit{D}}, \textbf{P-!-}Pki \rightarrow Qki >$ **P** defends itself uttering that the formula $Px \rightarrow Qx$ stands for ki. A new play equivalent to I_1 for X=**P** starts here

Move 5: $I_2 = <\textbf{\textit{CH}}, \text{O-!- Pki} >$
Move 6: $U_2 = <\textbf{\textit{CH}}, \text{P-?-ki}>$
Move 7: $U_3 = <\textbf{\textit{D}}, \text{O-!-Pki} \rightarrow \text{Qki} >$ A new play equivalent to I_1 for $X = \textbf{O}$ starts here
Move 8: $I_2 = <\textbf{\textit{CH}}, \text{P-!-Pki} >$ I_2 for $\textbf{P}$ is branching time (see Summary 3)

BRANCH 1	BRANCH 2
Move 9: $I_3 = <\textbf{\textit{CH}}, \text{O-!-Qki}>$	Null because **O** cannot attack an atomic formula.
Move 10: $I_3 = <\textbf{\textit{CH}}, \text{P-!-Qki} > ☺$	

Score
P wins by making the last move: the dialogue is *finished* and *closed*,   **O** can not move further, and the same atomic   formula appears in the moves: 9 and 10.

Note that in move 4 the proponent would have another option: to make the same move as O and the dialogue would have another order.

2) $\phi = Px \wedge Qx$

	O			**P**	
				$\forall x\,(Px \wedge Qx) \rightarrow \forall x\,(Px \wedge Qx)$	0
1	$\forall x\,(Px \wedge Qx)$	0		$\forall x\,(Px \wedge Qx)$	2
3	?-ki	2		Pki $\wedge$ Qki	6
5	Pki $\wedge$ Qki		1	?-ki	4

Branch **1**

	O			P	
				$\forall x(Px \wedge Qx) \rightarrow \forall x(Px \wedge Qx)$	0
1	$\forall x(Px \wedge Qx)$	0		$\forall x(Px \wedge Qx)$	2
3	?-ki	2		$Pki \wedge Qki$	6
5	$Pki \wedge Qki$		1	?-ki	4
7	$?-\wedge_2$	6		Qki ☺	10
9	Qki		5	$?-\wedge_2$	8

Branch **2**

	O			P	
				$\forall x(Px \wedge Qx) \rightarrow \forall x(Px \wedge Qx)$	0
1	$\forall x(Px \wedge Qx)$	0		$\forall x(Px \wedge Qx)$	2
3	?-ki	2		$Pki \wedge Qki$	6
5	$Pki \wedge Qki$		1	?-ki	4
7	$?-\wedge_1$	6		Pki ☺	10
9	Pki		5	$?-\wedge_1$	8

Move 0: $I_1 = < \tau , \textbf{P}\text{-!-}\forall x\,(Px \wedge Qx) \rightarrow \forall x(Px \wedge Qx) >$
Move 1: $I_2 = < \textbf{\textit{CH}}, \textbf{O}\text{-!-}\forall x(Px \wedge Qx) >$
A new play equivalent to U_1 for X=**O** starts here
Move 2: $I_3 = < \textbf{\textit{D}}, \textbf{P}\text{-!-}\forall x(Px \wedge Qx) >$
A new play equivalent to U_1 for X=**P** starts here
Move 3: $U_2 = < \textbf{\textit{CH}}, \textbf{O}\text{-?-ki} >$
Move 4: $U_2 = < \textbf{\textit{CH}}, \textbf{P}\text{-?-ki} >$
Move 5: $U_3 = < \textbf{\textit{D}}, \textbf{O}\text{-!-}Pki \wedge Qki >$
A new play equivalent to C_1 for X=**O** starts here
Move 6: $U_3 = < \textbf{\textit{D}}, \textbf{P}\text{-!-}Pki \wedge Qki >$

A new play equivalent to C_1 for X=P starts here
[C_1 for P is branching time (see *Summary 3*)]

BRANCH 1	BRANCH 2
Move 7: C_2=< *CH*, O-?-$\wedge_2$>	Move 7: C_2=< *CH*, O-?-$\wedge_1$>
Move 8: C_2=< *CH*, P-?-$\wedge_2$>	Move 8: C_2=< *CH*, P-?-$\wedge_1$>
Move 9: C_3=< *D*, O-!- Qki>	Move 9: C_3=< *D*, O-!- Pki>
Move 10: C_3=< *D*, P-!- Qki> ☺	Move 10 C_3=< *D*, P-!- Pki> ☺

Score
P wins by making the last moves:
the dialogical games are *finished* and *closed*,
O can not move further, and the same atomic
formula appears in moves 9 and 10 in both branches.

Case 22: $D(\exists x\phi \rightarrow \exists x\phi)$

	O			P	
				$\exists x\phi \rightarrow \exists x\phi$	0
1	$\exists x\phi$	0		$\exists x\phi$	2
3	?-$\exists$	2		$\phi[x/ki]$ ☺	6
5	$\phi[x/ki]$		1	?-$\exists$	4

Move 0: I_1=<τ, P-!-$\exists x\phi \rightarrow \exists x\phi$>
Move 1: I_2=< *CH*, O-!-$\exists x\phi$>
A new play equivalent to E_1 for X=O starts here
Move 2: I_3=< *D*, P-!-$\exists x\phi$>
A new play equivalent to E_1 for X=P starts here
Move 3: E_2=< *CH*, O-?-$\exists$>
Move 4: E_2=< *CH*, P-?-$\exists$>
P responds attacking the existential quantifier
Move 5: E_3=< *D*, O-!-$\phi[x/ki]$>
Move 6: E_3=< *D*, P-!-$\phi[x/ki]$> ☺

Score
P wins by making the last move:
the dialogue is *finished* and *closed*,
O can not move further, and the same atomic

formula appears in moves 5 and 6.

Below we show two specific cases, when φ= PxvQx, and when φ= Px.

1. φ= PxvQx

	O				P	
					∃x (PxvQx) →∃x (PxvQx)	0
1	∃x (PxvQx)	0			∃x (PxvQx)	2
3	?-∃	2			PkivQki	6
5	Pki vQki		1		?-∃	4

Branch 1

	O				P	
					∃x (PxvQx) →∃x (PxvQx)	0
1	∃x (PxvQx)	0			∃x (PxvQx)	2
3	?-∃	2			Pki vQki	6
5	PkivQki		1		?-∃	4
7	?-v	6			Qki ☺	10
9	Qki		5		?-v	8

Branch 2

	O				P	
					∃x(PxvQx) →∃x(PxvQx)	0
1	∃x(PxvQx)	0			∃x(PxvQx)	2
3	?-∃	2			Pki vQki	6
5	Pki vQki		1		?-∃	4
7	?-v	6			Pki ☺	10
9	Pki		5		?-v	8

Move 0: I₁=<τ, **P**-!-∃x(PxvQx) →∃x (PxvQx)>
Move 1: I₂=< **CH**, **O**-!-∃x(PxvQx)>   A new play equivalent to E₁ for X=**O** starts here

Move 2: $I_3 = < D, P-!-\exists x(Px \lor Qx)>$
A new play equivalent to E_1 for X=**P** starts here
Move 3: $E_2 = < \textbf{\textit{CH}}, O-?-\exists>$
Move 4: $E_2 = < \textbf{\textit{CH}}, P-?-\exists>$
Move 5: $E_3 = < D, O-!- Pki \lor Qki >$
A new play equivalent to D_1 for X=**O** starts here
Move 6: $E_3 = < D, P-!- Pki \lor Qki >$
A new play equivalent to D_1 for X=**P** starts here

Branching time

Branch 1:	Branch 2:
Move 7: $C_2 = < \textbf{\textit{CH}}, O-?-\lor>$	Move 7: $C_2 = < \textbf{\textit{CH}}, O-?-\lor>$
Move 8: $C_2 = < \textbf{\textit{CH}}, P-?-\lor>$	Move 8: $C_2 = < \textbf{\textit{CH}}, P-?-\lor>$
Move 9: $C_3 = < D, O-!- Qki>$	Move 9: $C_3 = < D, O-!- Pki>$
Move 10: $C_3 = < D, P-!- Qki>$	Move 10: $C_3 = < D, P-!- Pki>$

Score
P wins by making the last moves:
the dialogical games are *finished* and *closed,*
O can not move further, and the same atomic
formula appears in moves 9 and 10.

2. $\phi = Px$

	O			P	
				$\exists x\, Px \rightarrow \exists x\, Px$	0
1	$\exists xPx$	0		$\exists xPx$	2
3	?-∃	2		Pki ☺	6
5	Pki		1	?-∃	4

Move 0: $I_1 = <\tau, P-!-\exists xAx \rightarrow \exists xAx>$
Move 1: $I_2 = < \textbf{\textit{CH}}, O-!-\exists xAx>$
A new play equivalent to E_1 for X=**O** starts here
Move 2: $I_3 = < D, P-!-\exists xAx>$
A new play equivalent to E_1 for X=**P** starts here
Move 3: $E_2 = < \textbf{\textit{CH}}, O-?-\exists>$
Move 4: $E_2 = < \textbf{\textit{CH}}, P-?-\exists>$

	Move 5: E_3=< D, O-!-Pki>
	Move 6: E_3=< D, P-!- Pki > ☺

Score
P wins by making the last move:
the dialogue is *finished* and *closed,*
O can not move further, and the same atomic
formula appears in moves 5 and 6.

Case 23: D($\exists$xAx→$\forall$xAx)

	O			P	
				$\exists$xAx→$\forall$xAx	0
1	$\exists$xAx	0		$\forall$xAx	2
3	?-ki	2			
5	Akj ☺		1	?-$\exists$	4

(ki≠kj)

Move 0: I_1=<thesis, P-!-$\exists$xAx →$\forall$xAx>
Move 1: I_2=< *CH,* O-!-$\exists$xAx>   A new play equivalent to E_1 for X=O starts here
Move 2: I_3=< D, P-!-$\forall$xAx>   A new play equivalent to U_1 for X=P starts here
Move 3: U_2=< *CH,* O-?-ki>
Move 4: E_2=< *CH,* P-?-$\exists$>
Move 5: E_3=< D, O-!- Akj>   O introduces here a constant different from ki and so **P** will not be able to defend itself from the attack of move 3.
Score   **O wins** by making the last move: the dialogue is *finished* and *open,*   P can not move further, and no two positions feature the same atomic formula.

Case 24: $D(\forall x(Ax \rightarrow Bx) \rightarrow \exists x(Ax \rightarrow Bx))$

	O			P	
				$\forall x(Ax \rightarrow Bx) \rightarrow \exists x(Ax \rightarrow Bx)$	0
1	$\forall x(Ax \rightarrow Bx)$	0		$\exists x(Ax \rightarrow Bx)$	2
3	?-$\exists$	2		Aki$\rightarrow$Bki	4
5	Aki	4		Bki ☺	10
7	Aki$\rightarrow$Bki	1		?-ki	6
9	Bki	7		Aki	8

Move 0: I_1=<τ, P-!-$\forall x(Ax \rightarrow Bx) \rightarrow \exists x(Ax \rightarrow Bx)$>
Move 1: I_2=< *CH*, O-!-$\forall x(Ax \rightarrow Bx)$>   A new play equivalent to U_1 for X=O starts here
Move 2: I_3=< *D*, P-!-$\exists x(Ax \rightarrow Bx)$>   A new play equivalent to E_1 for X=P starts here
Move 3: E_2=< *CH*, O-?-$\exists$>
Move 4: E_3=< *D*, P-!-Aki$\rightarrow$Bki >   A new play equivalent to I_1 for X=P starts here
Move 5: I_2=< *CH*, O-!-Aki>
Move 6: U_2=< *CH*, P-?-ki >
Move 7: U_3=< *D*, O-!-Aki$\rightarrow$Bki>   A new play equivalent to I_1 for X=O starts here

Branch 1:	Branch 2:
Move 8: I_2=< *CH*, P-!-Aki >	Null because O cannot attack an atomic formula (Move 8)
Move 9: I_3=< *D*, O-!-Bki >	
Move 10: I_3=< *D*, P-!- Bki > ☺	

Score
P wins by making the last move: the dialogue is *finished* and *closed,*   O can not move further, and the same atomic   formula appears in moves 9 and 10.

Case 25: D($\forall$xAx$\rightarrow$$\exists$xAx)

	O			P	
				$\forall$xAx$\rightarrow$$\exists$xAx	0
1	$\forall$xAx	0		$\exists$xAx	2
3	?-$\exists$	2		Aki ☺	6
5	Aki		1	?-ki	4

Move 0: I_1=<τ, P-!-$\forall$xAx$\rightarrow$$\exists$xAx>
Move 1: I_2=< *CH*, O-!-$\forall$xAx>   A new play equivalent to U_1 for X=**O** starts here
Move 2: I_3=< *D*, P-!-$\exists$xAx>   A new play equivalent to E_1 for X=**P** starts here
Move 3: E_2=< *CH*, O-?-$\exists$>
Move 4: U_2=< *CH*, P-?-ki >
Move 5: U_3=< *D*, O-!- Aki>
Move 6: E_3=< *D*, P-!- Aki > ☺
Score   **P wins** by making the last move: the dialogue is *finished* and *closed,*   O can not move further, and the same atomic   formula appears in moves 5 and 6.

Case 26: D(Aki$\rightarrow$$\forall$xAx)

	O			P	
				Aki$\rightarrow$$\forall$xAx	0
1	Aki	0		$\forall$xAx	2
3	?-kj ☺	2			

Move 0: I_1=<τ, P-!- Ac$\rightarrow$$\forall$xAx >
Move 1: I_2=< *CH*, O-!-Aki >
Move 2: I_3=< *D*, P-!-$\forall$xAx>   A new play equivalent to U_1 for X=**P** starts here
Move 3: U_2=< *CH*, O-?-ki > ☺

O asks here for a cosntant diferent from ki and so **P** will not be able to defend itself from the attack (see case 23)		

Score
O wins by making the last move:
the dialogue is *finished* and *open*,
P can not move further, and no two positions feature the same atomic
formula.

Case 27: $D(Pki \rightarrow \exists xPx)$

	O			P	
				$Pki \rightarrow \exists xPx$	0
1	Pki	0		$\exists xPx$	2
3	?-∃	2		Pki ☺	4

Move 0: $I_1 = <\tau$, **P**-!-$Pki \rightarrow \exists xPx>$
Move 1: $I_2 = <$ **CH**, **O**-!- Pki $>$
Move 2: $I_3 = <$ **D**, **P**-!-$\exists xPx>$ A new play equivalent to E_1 for X=**P** starts here
Move 3: $E_2 = <$ **CH**, **O**-?-∃$>$
Move 4: $E_3 = <$ **D**, **P**-!-Pki$>$
Score **P wins** by making the last move: the dialogue is *finished* and *closed*, **O** can not move further, and the same atomic formula appears in moves 1 and 4.

Case 28: $D(\forall x(Ax \rightarrow Bx) \rightarrow \exists x(Ax \wedge Bx))$

	O			P	
				$\forall x(Ax \rightarrow Bx) \rightarrow \exists x(Ax \wedge Bx)$	0
1	$\forall x(Ax \rightarrow Bx)$	0		$\exists x(Ax \wedge Bx)$	2
3	?-∃	2		$Aki \wedge Bki$	4

Branch 1

5	?-∧₁	4			
7	Aki→Bki ☺		1	?-ki	6

Branch 2

5	?-∧₂	4			
7	Aki→Bki ☺		1	?-ki	6

Move 0: I_1=<τ, P-!-$\forall x(Ax \rightarrow Bx) \rightarrow \exists x(Ax \wedge Bx)$>
Move 1: I_2=< *CH*, O-!-$\forall x(Ax \rightarrow Bx)$>   A new play equivalent to U_1 for X=O starts here
Move 2: I_3=< *D*, P-!-$\exists x(Ax \wedge Bx)$>   A new play equivalent to E_1 for X=P starts here
Move 3: E_2=< *CH*, O-?-$\exists$>
Move 4: E_3=< *D*, P-!-Aki $\wedge$ Bki >   A new play equivalent to C_1 for X=P starts here

Branching time

BRANCH 1	BRANCH 2
Move 5: I_2=< *CH*, O-!-?-∧₁>	Move 5: I_2=< *CH*, O-!-?-∧₂>
Move 6: U_2=< *CH*, P-?-$\forall x/c$>	Move 6: U_2=< *CH*, P-?-$\forall x/c$>
Move 7: U_3=< *D*, O-!-Aki $\rightarrow$ Bki > A new play equivalent to I_1 for X=O ☺ starts here	Move 7: U_3=< *D*, O-!-Aki $\rightarrow$ Bki > A new play equivalent to I_1 for X=O ☺ starts here

Score
O wins by making the last move: the dialogue is *finished* and *open*,   **P** can not move further, and no two positions feature the same atomic formula.

Case 29: $D(\exists x(Ax \wedge Bx) \rightarrow (\exists xAx \wedge \exists xBx))$

	O			P	
				$\exists x(Ax \wedge Bx) \rightarrow (\exists xAx \wedge \exists xBx)$	0
1	$\exists x(Ax \wedge Bx)$	0		$(\exists xAx \wedge \exists xBx)$	2

Branch 1

	O			P	
				$\exists x(Ax \wedge Bx) \rightarrow (\exists xAx \wedge \exists xBx)$	0
1	$\exists x(Ax \wedge Bx)$	0		$(\exists xAx \wedge \exists xBx)$	2
3	$?\text{-}\wedge_1$	2		$\exists xAx$	4
5	$?\text{-}\exists$	4		Aki ☺	10
7	$Aki \wedge Bki$	1		$?\text{-}\exists$	6
9	Aki	7		$?\text{-}\wedge_1$	8

Branch 2

	O			P	
				$\exists x(Ax \wedge Bx) \rightarrow (\exists xAx \wedge \exists xBx)$	0
1	$\exists x(Ax \wedge Bx)$	0		$(\exists xAx \wedge \exists xBx)$	2
3	$?\text{-}\wedge_2$	2		$\exists xAx$	4
5	$?\text{-}\exists$	4		Bki ☺	10
7	$Aki \wedge Bki$	1		$?\text{-}\exists$	6
9	Bki	7		$?\text{-}\wedge_2$	8

Move 0: $I_1 = <\tau, P\text{-}!\text{-}\exists x(Ax \wedge Bx) \rightarrow (\exists xAx \wedge \exists xBx)>$
Move 1: $I_2 = <\textbf{\textit{CH}}, O\text{-}!\text{-}\exists x(Ax \wedge Bx)>$ A new play equivalent to E_1 for X=O starts here
Move 2: $I_3 = <\textbf{\textit{D}}, P\text{-}!\text{-}(\exists xAx \wedge \exists xBx)>$ A new play equivalent to C_1 for X=P starts here

Branching time	
Branch 1	**Branch 2**

Move 3 : C_2=< CH, O-?-$\wedge_1$>	Move 3: C_2=< CH, O-?-$\wedge_2$>
Move 4: C_3=< D, P-!-$\exists$xAx> A new play equivalent to E_1 for X=P starts here	Move 4: C_3=< D, P-!-$\exists$xBx> A new play equivalent to E_1 for X=P starts here
Move 5: E_2=< CH, O-?-$\exists$>	Move 5: E_2=< CH, O-?-$\exists$>
Move 6: E_2=< CH, P-?-$\exists$>	Move 6: E_2=< CH, P-?-$\exists$>
Move 7: E_3=< D, O-!-Aki$\wedge$Bki> A new play equivalent to C_1 for X=O starts here	Move 7: E_3=< D, O-!-Aki$\wedge$Bki> A new play equivalent to C_1 for X=O starts here
Move 8: C_2=< CH, P-?-$\wedge_1$>	Move 8: C_2=< CH, P-?-$\wedge_2$>
Move 9: C_3=< D, O-!-Aki>	Move 9: C_3=< D, O-!-Bki>
Move 10: E_3=< D, P-!-Aki>	Move 10: E_3=< D, P-!-Bki>

Score
O wins by making the last move: the dialogue is *finished* and *open*, **P** can not move further, and no two positions feature the same atomic formula.

Case 30: $D(\exists x(Ax \rightarrow \forall xAx))$

	O			P	
				$\exists x(Ax \rightarrow \forall xAx)$	0
1	?-$\exists$	0		Aki$\rightarrow\forall$xAx	2
3	Aki	2		$\forall$xAx	4
5	?-kj	4		Akj ☻	8
				Akj$\rightarrow\forall$xAx	6
7	Akj	6			

Move 0: E_1=<τ, P-!-$\exists$x(Ax$\rightarrow\forall$xAx)>
Move 1: E_2=< CH, O-?-$\exists$>
Move 2: E_3=<D, P-!- Aki$\rightarrow\forall$xAx > A new play equivalent to I_1 for X=P starts here
Move 3: I_2=< CH, O-!-Aki>
Move 4: I_3=< D, P-!-$\forall$xAx>

A new play equivalent to U_1 for X=**P** starts here
Move 5: U_2=< *CH*, O-?-kj>
With intuitionistic rules the dialogue finishes here
Move 6: E_3=< *D*, **P**-!- Akj→∀xAx>
A new play equivalent to I_1 for X=**P** starts here
Move 7: I_2=< *CH*, O-!-Akj>
Move 8: U_3=< *D*, **P**-!-Akj>
S c o r e **P wins** by making the last move: the dialogue is *finished* and *closed*, O can not move further, and the same atomic formula appears in moves 1 and 4.

Case 31: $D(\forall x(Ax \lor Bx) \to (\forall xAx \lor \forall xBx))$

	O			P	
				$\forall x(Ac \lor Bc) \to (\forall xAx \lor \forall xBx)$	0
1	$\forall x(Ax \lor Bx)$	0		$(\forall xAx \lor \forall xBx)$	2
3	?-$\lor$	2		$\forall xAx$	4
5	?-ki	4			
7	Aki$\lor$Bki		1	?-ki	6
			7	?$\lor$	8
			Branch 1		
				$\forall x(Ac \lor Bc) \to (\forall xAx \lor \forall xBx)$	0
1	$\forall x(Ax \lor Bx)$	0		$(\forall xAx \lor \forall xBx)$	2
3	?-$\lor$	2		$\forall xAx$	4
5	?-ki	4		Aki	10
7	Aki$\lor$Bki		1	?-ki	6
9	Aki		7	?$\lor$	8
			Branch 2		
				$\forall x(Ac \lor Bc) \to (\forall xAx \lor \forall xBx)$	0
1	$\forall x(Ax \lor Bx)$	0		$(\forall xAx \lor \forall xBx)$	2
3	?-$\lor$	2		$\forall xAx$	4
5	?-ki	4			
7	Aki$\lor$Bki		1	?-ki	6
9	Bki		7	?$\lor$	8
				$\forall xBx$	10
11	?-kj	10			

Move 0: $I_1 = \langle \tau,$ **P**-!-$\forall x(Ac \lor Bc) \to (\forall xAx \lor \forall xBx)\rangle$
Move 1: $I_2 = \langle$ ***CH***, **O**-!-$\forall x(Ac \lor Bc)\rangle$ A new play equivalent to U_1 for X=**O** starts here
Move 2: $I_3 = \langle$ ***D***, **P**-!-$(\forall xAx \lor \forall xBx)\rangle$ A new play equivalent to D_1 for X=**P** starts here
Move 3: $D_2 = \langle$ ***CH***, **O**-?-$\lor\rangle$

Move 4: $D_3 = <D, P\text{-!-}\forall x Ax>$
A new play equivalent to U_1 for X=**P** starts here
Move 5: $U_2 = <CH, O\text{-?-}ki>$
Move 6: $U_2 = <CH, P\text{-?-}ki>$
Move 7: $U_3 = <D, O\text{- !- } Aki \lor Bki >$
A new play equivalent to D_1 for X=**O** starts here

Branching time

Branch 1	Branch 2
Move 8: $D_2 = <CH, P\text{-?-}\lor>$	Move 8: $D_2 = <CH, P\text{-?-}\lor>$
Move 9: $D_3 = <D, O\text{-!-}Aki>$	Move 9: $D_3 = <D, O\text{-!-}Bki>$
Move 10: $D_3 = <D, P\text{-!-}Aki>$	Move 10: $D_3 = <D, P\text{-!-}\forall x Bx>$
	A new play equivalent to U_1 for X=**P** starts here
	Move 11: $U_2 = <CH, O\text{-?-}kj>$

Score
O wins by making the last move:
the dialogue is *finished* and *open*,
P can not move further, and no two positions feature the same atomic formula.

Note: If the dialogue had consisted only in the branch 1, **P** would have won.

Case 32: D(¬∃xAx→∀x¬Ax)

	O			P	
				¬∃xAx→∀x¬Ax	0
1	¬∃xAx	0		∀x¬Ax	2
3	?-ki	2		¬Aki	4
5	Aki	4			
			1	∃xAx	6
7	?-∃	6		Aki ☺	8

Move 0: I₁=<τ, P-!- ¬∃xAx→∀x¬Ax >
Move 1: I₂=< *CH*, O-!- ¬∃xAx > A new play equivalent to N₁ for X=O starts here
Move 2: I₃=< *D*, P-!-∀x¬Ax > A new play equivalent to U₁ for X=P starts here
Move 3: U₂=< *CH*, O-?-ki>
Move 4: U₃=< *D*, P-!-¬Aki> A new play equivalent to N₁ for X=P starts here
Move 5: N₂=< *CH*, O- !-Aki >
Move 6: N₂=< *CH*, P- !- ∃xAx> A new play equivalent to E₁ for X=P starts here
Move 7: E₂=< *CH*, O-?-∃>
Move 8: E₃=< *D*, P-!-Aki>
Score **P wins** by making the last move: the dialogue is *finished* and *closed*, O can not move further, and the same atomic formula appears in moves 5 and 8.

Case 33: D(∀xAx→Aki) (Specification)

	O			P	
				∀xAx→Aki	0
1	∀xAx	0		Aki ☺	4
3	Aki		1	?-ki	2

Move 0: $I_1 = <\tau, \mathbf{P}\text{-!-}\forall xAx \rightarrow Aki >$
Move 1: $I_2 = <\mathbf{\mathit{CH}}, \mathbf{O}\text{-!-}\forall xAx >$ A new play equivalent to U_1 for X=$\mathbf{O}$ starts here
Move 2: $U_2 = <\mathbf{\mathit{D}}, \mathbf{P}\text{-?-}ki>$
Move 3: $U_3 = <\mathbf{\mathit{CH}}, \mathbf{O}\text{-!-}Aki >$
Move 4: $I_3 = <\mathbf{\mathit{D}}, \mathbf{P}\text{-!-} Aki >$
Score **P wins** by making the last move: the dialogue is *finished* and *closed,* **O** can not move further, and the same atomic formula appears in moves 3 and 4.

Case 34: $D(\forall xAx \rightarrow \neg\exists x \neg Ax)$

	O			**P**	
				$\forall xAx \rightarrow \neg\exists x \neg Ax$	0
1	$\forall xAx$	0		$\neg\exists x \neg Ax$	2
3	$\exists x \neg Ax$	2			
5	$\neg Aki$		3	?-∃	4
7	Aki		1	?-ki	6
	-		5	Aki ☺	8

Move 0: $I_1 = <\tau, \mathbf{P}\text{-!-}\forall xAx \rightarrow \neg\exists x \neg Ax>$
Move 1: $I_2 = <\mathbf{\mathit{CH}}, \mathbf{O}\text{-!-}\forall xAx>$ A new play equivalent to U_1 for X=$\mathbf{O}$ starts here
Move 2: $I_3 = <\mathbf{\mathit{D}}, \mathbf{P}\text{-!-} \neg\exists x \neg Ax>$ A new play equivalent to N_1 for X=$\mathbf{P}$ starts here
Move 3: $N_2 = <\mathbf{\mathit{CH}}, \mathbf{O}\text{-!-} \exists x \neg Ax >$ A new play equivalent to E_1 for X=$\mathbf{O}$ starts here
Move 4: $E_2 = <\mathbf{\mathit{CH}}, \mathbf{P}\text{-?-}∃>$
Move 5: $E_3 = <\mathbf{\mathit{D}}, \mathbf{O}\text{-!-} \neg Aki>$ A new play equivalent to N_1 for X=$\mathbf{O}$ starts here
Move 6: $U_2 = <\mathbf{\mathit{CH}}, \mathbf{P}\text{-?-}ki>$

Move 7: $U_3=< D, O\text{-!-}Aki>$
Move 8: $N_2=< D, P\text{-!-}Aki>$ ☺

Score
P wins by making the last move:
the dialogue is *finished* and *closed*,
O can not move further, and the same atomic
formula appears in moves 7 and 8.

Case 35: $D(\forall x(Ax\to Bx)\land(\exists x\neg Bx))\to(\exists x\neg Ax))$

	O			P	
				$(\forall x(Ax\to Bx)\land(\exists x\neg Bx))\to(\exists x\neg Ax)$	0
1	$\forall x(Ax\to Bx)\land(\exists x\neg Bx)$	0		$\exists x\neg Ax$	2
3	?-∃	2		¬Aki	10
5	$\forall x(Ax\to Bx)$		1	?-$\land_1$	4
7	$\exists x\neg Bx$		1	?-$\land_2$	6
9	¬Bki		7	?-∃	8
11	Aki	10			
13	Aki→Bki		5	?-ki	12
15	Bki		13	Aki	14
			9	Bki ☺	16

Move 0: $I_1=<\tau, P\text{-!-} (\forall x(Ax\to Bx)\land(\exists x\neg Bx))\to(\exists x\neg Ax)>$
Move 1: $I_2=< CH, O\text{-!-}\forall x(Ax\to Bx)\land(\exists x\neg Bx)>$
A new play equivalent to C_1 for X=O starts here
Move 2: $I_3=< D, P\text{-!-}\exists x\neg Ax >$
A new play equivalent to E_1 for X=P starts here
Move 3: $E_2=< CH, O\text{- ?-}\exists>$
Move 4: $C_2=< CH, P\text{-?-}\land_1>$
Move 5: $C_3=< D, O\text{-!-}\forall x(Ax\to Bx)>$
A new play equivalent to U_1 for X=O starts here
Move 6: $C_2=< CH, P\text{-?-}\land_2>$
Move 7: $C_3=< D, O\text{-!-}(\exists x\neg Bx)>$
A new play equivalent to E_1 for X=O starts here

Move 8: $E_2 = <$ *CH*, P- ?-∃ $>$
Move 9: $E_3 = < D$, O- !- ¬Bki$>$ A new play equivalent to N_1 for X=O starts here
Move 10: $E_3 = < D$, P- !- ¬Aki$>$ A new play equivalent to N_1 for X=P starts here
Move 11: $N_2 = <$ *CH*, O-!- Aki$>$
Move 12: $U_2 = <$ *CH*, P- ?-ki$>$
Move 13: $U_3 = < D$, O-!-Aki→Bki $>$ A new play equivalent to I_1 pour X=O starts here

Branching time

Branch 1	Branch 2
Move 14: $I_2 = <$ *CH*, P-!-Aki$>$	Null because O cannot attack an atomic formula (Move 8)
Move 15: $I_3 = < D$, O-!- Bki$>$	
Move 16: $N_2 = <$ *CH*, P-!-Bki$>$	

Score

P wins by making the last move:
the dialogue is *finished* and *closed,*
O can not move further, and the same atomic
formula appears in moves 15 and 16.

Case 36: $D(\forall x(Ax \lor Bx) \land \exists x \neg Ax) \rightarrow (\exists xBx))$

	O			P	
				$(\forall x(Ax \lor Bx) \land \exists x \neg Ax) \rightarrow (\exists xBx)$	0
1	$\forall x(Ax \lor Bx) \land \exists x \neg Ax$	0		$\exists xBx$	2
3	?-$\exists$	2			
5	$\forall x(Ax \lor Bx)$	1		?-$\land_1$	4
7	$\exists x \neg Ax$	1		?-$\land_2$	6
9	$\neg Aki$	7		?-$\exists$	8
11	$Aki \lor Bki$	5		?-ki	10
13		11		?-$\lor$	12

Branch 1

	O			P	
11	$Aki \lor Bki$	5		?-ki	10
13	Bki	11		?-$\lor$	12
			9	Bki ☺	14

Branch 2

	O			P	
11	$Aki \lor Bki$	5		?-ki	10
13	Aki	11		?-$\lor$	12
			9	Aki ☺	14

Move 0: $I_1 = <\tau, P\text{-}!\text{-}(\forall x(Ax \lor Bx) \land \exists x \neg Ax) \rightarrow (\exists xBx)>$
Move 1: $I_2 = <$ *CH*, $O\text{-}!\text{-}(\forall x(Ax \lor Bx) \land \exists x \neg Ax)>$ A new play equivalent to C_1 for X=**O** starts here
Move 2: $I_3 = <$ *D*, $P\text{-}!\text{-} \exists xBx>$ A new play equivalent to E_1 for X=**P** starts here
Move 3: $E_2 = <$ *CH*, $O\text{-}?\text{-}\exists>$
Move 4: $C_2 = <$ *CH*, $P\text{-}?\text{-}\land_1>$
Move 5: $C_3 = <$ *D*, $O\text{-}!\text{-} \forall x(Ax \lor Bx)>$ A new play equivalent to U_1 for X=**O** starts here
Move 6: $C_2 = <$ *CH*, $P\text{-}?\text{-}\land_2>$
Move 7: $C_3 = <$ *D*, $O\text{-}!\text{-} \exists x \neg Ax>$

A new play equivalent to E_1 for X=O starts here
Move 8: E_2=< *CH*, P-?-∃>
Move 9: E_3=< *D*, O-!- ¬Aa>
A new play equivalent to N_1 for X=O starts here
Move 10: U_2=< *CH*, P-?-ki>
Move 11: U_3=< *D*, O-!- Aki∨Bki >
A new play equivalent to D_1 for X=O starts here

Branching time

Branch 1	Branch 2
Move 12: D_2=< *CH*, P-?-∨>	Move 12: D_2=< *CH*, P-?-∨>
Move 13: D_3=< *D*, O-!- Bki>	Move 13: D_3=< *D*, O-!- Aki>
Move 14: E_3=< *D*, P-!- Bki>	Move 14: N_2=< *CH*, P- !- Aki >

Score
P wins by making the last moves: the dialogical games are *finished* and *closed*, O can not move further, and the same atomic formula appears in moves 13 and 14.

Case 37: D($\forall x\forall yRxy \rightarrow \forall x\forall yRyx$)

	O			P	
				($\forall x\forall yRxy \rightarrow \forall x\forall yRyx$)	0
1	$\forall x\forall yRxy$	0		$\forall x\forall yRyx$	2
3	?-ki	2		$\forall yRxki$	4
5	?-kj	4		Rkjki ☺	10
7	$\forall yRkjy$		1	?-kj	6
9	Rkjki		7	?-ki	8

Move 0: I_1−<τ, **P**-!- ($\forall x\forall yRxy \rightarrow \forall x\forall yRyx$)>
Move 1: I_2=< *CH*, O-!- $\forall x\forall yRxy$ >
A new play equivalent to U_1 for X=O starts here
Move 2: I_3=< *D*, P-!- $\forall x\forall yRyx$ >
A new play equivalent to U_1 for X=P starts here

Move 3: $U_2 = <$ **CH**, O-?-ki$>$
Move 4: $U_3 = <$ **D**, P-!-$\forall y R y k i$ $>$ A new play equivalent to U_1 for X=**P** starts here
Move 5: $U_2 = <$ **CH**, O-?-kj$>$
Move 6: $U_2 = <$ **CH**, P-?-kj$>$
Move 7: $U_3 = <$ **D**, O-!-$\forall y R k j y >$ A new play equivalent to U_1 for X=**O** starts here
Move 8: $U_2 = <$ **CH**, P-?-ki$>$
Move 9: $U_3 = <$ **D**, O-!-Rkjki$>$
Move 10: $U_3 = <$ **D**, P-!-Rkjki$>$
S c o r e   **P wins** by making the last move: the dialogue is *finished* and *closed*,   **O** can not move further, and the same atomic   formula appears in moves 9 and 10.

Case 38: D($\exists y \forall x A x y \rightarrow \forall x \exists y A x y$)

	O			P	
				$\exists y \forall x A x y \rightarrow \forall x \exists y A x y$	0
1	$\exists y \forall x A x y$	0		$\forall x \exists y A x y$	2
3	?-ki	2		$\exists y A k i y$	4
5	?-$\exists$	4		$A k i k j$ ☺	10
7	$\forall x A x k j$		1	?-$\exists$	6
9	$A k i k j$		7	?-ki	8

Move 0: $I_1 = <\tau$, P-!- $\exists y \forall x A x y \rightarrow \forall x \exists y A x y$ $>$
Move 1: $I_2 = <$ **CH**, O-!- $\exists y \forall x A x y >$ A new play equivalent to E_1 for X=**O** starts here
Move 2: $I_3 = <$ **D**, P-!-$\forall x \exists y A x y$ $>$ A new play equivalent to U_1 for X=**P** starts here
Move 3: $U_2 = <$ **CH**, O-?-ki$>$
Move 4: $U_3 = <$ **D**, P-!-$\exists y A k i y$ $>$ A new play equivalent to E_1 for X=**P** starts here

Move 5: $E_2 = <\mathit{CH}, O\text{-?-}\exists>$
Move 6: $E_2 = <\mathit{CH}, P\text{-?-}\exists>$
Move 7: $E_3 = <\mathit{D}, O\text{-!-} \forall xAxkj>$ A new play equivalent to U_1 for $X=O$ starts here
Move 8: $U_2 = <\mathit{CH}, P\text{-?-ki}>$
Move 9: $U_3 = <\mathit{D}, O\text{-!-Akikj}>$
Move 10: $E_3 = <\mathit{D}, P\text{-!-Akikj}>$
Score   **P wins** by making the last move: the dialogue is *finished* and *closed,*   O can not move further, and the same atomic   formula appears in moves 9 and 10.

Case 39: $D(\forall x(\forall xAx \rightarrow Ax) \rightarrow \forall xAx)$

	O			P	
				$\forall x(\forall xAx \rightarrow Ax) \rightarrow \forall xAx$	0
1	$\forall x(\forall xAx \rightarrow Ax)$	0		$\forall xAx$	2
3	?-ki	2			
5	$\forall xAx \rightarrow Aki$		1	?-ki	4
			5	$\forall xAx$	6

Option 1:

Branch 1

↳	O			P	
				$\forall x(\forall xAx \rightarrow Ax) \rightarrow \forall xAx$	0
1	$\forall x(\forall xAx \rightarrow Ax)$	0		$\forall xAx$	2
3	?-ki	2		Aki ☺	8
5	$\forall xAx \rightarrow Aki$		1	?-ki	4
7	Aki		5	$\forall xAx$	6

Branch 2

↳	O			P	
				$\forall x(\forall xAx \rightarrow Ax) \rightarrow \forall xAx$	0
1	$\forall x(\forall xAx \rightarrow Ax)$	0		$\forall xAx$	2
3	?-ki	2			
5	$\forall xAx \rightarrow Aki$		1	?-ki	4
			5	$\forall xAx$	6
7	?-kj	6			
9	$\forall xAx \rightarrow Akj$		1	?-kj	8
			9	$\forall xAx$	10
11	?-kz	10			
			1	?-kz	12
				$\rightarrow \infty$	

Option 2:

Branch 1

↳	O				P	
					$\forall x(\forall xAx \rightarrow Ax) \rightarrow \forall xAx$	0
1	$\forall x(\forall xAx \rightarrow Ax)$	0			$\forall xAx$	2
3	?-ki	2			Aki☺	8
5	$\forall xAx \rightarrow Aki$		1		?-ki	4
7	Aki		5		$\forall xAx$	6

Branch 2

↳	O				P	
					$\forall x(\forall xAx \rightarrow Ax) \rightarrow \forall xAx$	0
1	$\forall x(\forall xAx \rightarrow Ax)$	0			$\forall xAx$	2
3	?-ki	2				
5	$\forall xAx \rightarrow Aki$		1		?-ki	4
			5		$\forall xAx$	6
7	?-ki	6				
9	$\forall xAx \rightarrow Aki$				?-ki	8
			9		$\forall xAx$	10
11	?-ki	10				

Move 0: $I_1 = <\tau,$ **P**-!- $(\forall x(\forall xAx \rightarrow Ax) \rightarrow \forall xAx)>$
Move 1: $I_2 = <$ ***CH,*** **O**-!- $\forall x(\forall xAx \rightarrow Ax)>$ A new play equivalent to U_1 for $X=$**O** starts here
Move 2: $I_3 = <$ ***D,*** **P**-!- $\forall xAx>$ A new play equivalent to U_1 for $X=$**P** starts here
Move 3: $U_2 = <$ ***CH,*** **O**-?-ki>
Move 4: $U_2 = <$ ***CH,*** **P**-?-ki>
Move 5: $U_3 = <$ ***D,*** **O**-!-$(\forall xAx \rightarrow Aki)>$ A new play equivalent to I_1 for $X=$**O** starts here
Move 6: $I_2 = <$ ***CH,*** **P**- !- $\forall xAx>$ A new play equivalent to U_1 for $X=$**P** starts here

After move 6 there is a branching with two options for **O** of attacking the universal quantifier: to choose the same (option 2) or different constant (option 1).

Option 1	Option 2
Move 7 : $U_2 = <$ ***CH,*** **O**-?-kj>	Move 7: $U_2 = <$ ***CH,*** **O**-?-ki>
Move 8: $U_2 = <$ ***CH,*** **P**-?-kj>	**O** attacks the move 6 with the
Move 9: $U_3 = <$ ***D,*** **O**-!-$(\forall xAx \rightarrow Akj)>$ A new play equivalent to I_1 for $X=$**O** starts here	same constant ki already chosen in move 3. **P** cannot respond by attacking move 1 with ki once more be-
Move 10: $I_2 = <$ ***CH,*** **P**- !- $\forall xAx>$	cause the rank 2 has been used up
Move 11: $U_2 = <$ ***CH,*** **O**-?-kz>	(RS-5).
Move 12: $U_2 = <$ ***CH,*** **P**-?-kz>	
$\rightarrow \infty$	
Here **O** attacked with a different constant and **P**, taking advantage of this, extends the game indefinitely by repeating the attack against Move 1. Indeed, using a different constant (but not a new one), **P** did not make a strict repetition of an attack.	

Score   **O** wins in both.   In option 2, **O wins** by making the last move:

the dialogue is *finished* and *open*,
P can not move further, and no two positions feature the same atomic
formula.
In option 1, O wins because the dialogue doesn't finish and never closed.

Case 40: D(¬∀x∃xAxy)

O			P	
			¬∀x∃xAxy	0
1	∀x∃xAxy	0		
3	∃xAxki	1	?-ki	2
		3	?-∃	4

Branch 1

O			P	
			¬∀x∃xAxy	0
1	∀x∃xAxy	0		
3	∃xAxki	1	?-ki	2
5	Akjki	3	?-∃	4
7	∃xAxkj	1	?-kj	6
9	Akzkj	7	?-∃	8
		1	?-kz	10
			→∞	

Branch 2

O			P	
			¬∀x∃xAxy	0
1	∀x∃xAxy	0		
3	∃xAxki	1	?-ki	2
5	Akiki	3	?-∃	4

Move 0: $N_1 = <\tau$, P-!-$(\neg\forall x\exists xAxy)>$

Move 1: $N_2 = <$ *CH*, O-!- $\forall x\exists xAxy)>$ A new play equivalent to U_1 for X=O starts here

Move 2: $U_2 = <$ *CH*, P-?-ki$>$

Move 3: $U_3 = <$ *D*, O-!-$(\exists xAxki)>$ A new play equivalent to E_1 for X=O starts here

Move 4: $E_2 = <$ *CH*, P- ?- $\exists>$

In the next move O has two options: to defend itself by choosing the same constant ki (option 2) or a different one (option 1).

Option 1	Option 2
Move 5: $E_3 = <$ *D*, O-!- Akjki$>$	Move 5: $E_3 = <$ *D*, O-!- Akiki$>$
Move 6: $U_2 = <$ *CH*, P-?-kj$>$	
Move 7: $U_3 = <$ *D*, O-!-$(\exists xAxkj)>$ A new play equivalent to E_1 for X=O starts here	
Move 8: $E_2 = <$ *CH*, P- ?- $\exists>$	
Move 9: $E_3 = <$ *D*, O-!- Akzkj$>$	
Move 10: $U_2 = <$ *CH*, P-?-kz$>$	
$\rightarrow \infty$	

Score   O wins in both.   In option 2, **O wins** by making the last move: the dialogue is *finished* and *open,*   P can not move further, and no two positions feature the same atomic formula.   In option 1, O wins because the dialogue doesn't finish and never closed.

PROPOSITIONAL-MODAL-DIALOGICAL LOGIC

Introduction[16]

The propositional modal language is an extension of the pure propositional classical language by adding new 1-ary connectives (known as the necessity and the possibility connectives or more abstract as box ($\Box$) and diamond ($\Diamond$) connectives).

In basic modal logic, box and diamond are interdefinable:

$$\Box\varphi \text{ iff } \neg\Diamond\neg\varphi$$
$$\Diamond\varphi \text{ iff } \neg\Box\neg\varphi$$

Unlike the propositional connectives of classical logic, box and diamond do not have a uniform and fixed interpretation. In fact, different readings of these connectives suggest different semantics and proof systems. E.g.:

$\Box$:	$\Diamond$:
φ is known	$\neg\varphi$: φ is not known
φ is necessary	φ is possible
φ will be always true	φ will be someday true
φ was always true	φ was someday true
φ is obligatory	φ is permissible
φ is provable	φ is consistent (with some formal system of arithmetic)

In these readings, it should be clear, at least from the first four pairs of the list, that they are intended as kinds of quantifiers over information states (or scenarios), possible worlds and over time contexts. Modal languages have been also used to analyze behavior of computer programs and the state transitions of (finite) automata. Furthermore, many modal languages such as temporal languages combine the different readings of the modal connectives.

---

[16] Rahman, Shahid. *Frames and Validity.* Unpublished manuscript.

Modal logic had an important place in Aristotle's *Organon*. In fact, two thirds of the *Analytica Priora* deal with modal logic. Despite some developments by the Stoics and intensive discussions in the Middle Ages it had far less influence than assertoric syllogistics. Perhaps this is because of the many philosophical and logical issues involved. It's interesting to note that in the Buddhist and Jaina tradition, and in general in the Indian tradition, modal logic occupied the center of the philosophical reflections; and this seems to be also the case of the Arabic tradition (especially in the work of Avicenna), but somehow these traditions got lost.

The first developments and applications of modal logic were philosophical and connected to various philosophical notions of necessity (sometimes identified with the temporal reading of the box). The first attempts to formalise modal logic by the end of the 19th century within the algebraic style of these times were penned by the French logician of Scottish origin Hugh MacColl (1837-1909), and were overtaken and axiomatised by Clarence Irving Lewis by 1918. In fact, after the publication of Whitehead and Russell's *Principia Mathematica* (1910-1912), the logistic methods of presenting a logic as a set of axioms closed under a consequence relation replaced rapidly the algebraic methods of calculation of the 19th century. MacColl's modal logic was formulated in the algebraic framework and Lewis recasted MacColl modal algebraic calculus, including MacColl's definition of strict implication, in the logistic language developed by Frege, Peano and others. Sadly, in later life Lewis seemed to take great care to hide the traces leading to the origins of strict implication and modal logic as they are presented in his joint work with Langford (1932). MacColl's several attempts at systematic presentation of his logic do not satisfy modern standards of rigour. MacColl hesitates between a (relational and) many valued and an explicit approach to modal logic – the latter characterized by the introduction of modal operators which bind propositional formulae in the object language. Still, his work clarifies what his algebra contains, and as pinpointed by Hughes and Creswell (1968) and Read (1999), what is harder to ascertain is what it does not contain.[17] Stephen Read (1999), presented the first thorough and systematic reconstruction of MacColl's modal logic within the framework of a modal algebra with strict implication which yields what we

---

[17] Hughes/Cresswell 1968, p. 214 n.

nowadays call the normal modal logic **T**.[18] MacColl is not only the father of strict implication, he is also the father of logical pluralism and explores some ideas which could be seen as the origins of the reflection on the logic of relevance and free logic.

As early as 1946 Carnap explored the idea of analysing modality as quantification over possible worlds, but he did not have the relation of accessibility which defines possible world semantics. The nowadays possible world semantics of modal logic was born by the confluence of the model theoretical approach to formal semantics of the polish tradition with the axiomatics of Lewis and followers. Actually there was another link less visible but also very important, namely link between the already mentioned algebraic logic and the model-theoretical approach to the semantics of modal logic. This link is a result of Stephen Kanger achieved in his seminars at the University of Stockholm by 1955 and published 1957 by that university under the title *Provability in Logic*; and of Richard Montague. Indeed, in a lecture of 1955 at the UCLA Montague gave a full model theoretical interpretation of propositional modal logic.. Kanger referred in a footnote (1957c, 39) to the work of Jónnson and Tarski (1951), from whose his use of the relational apparatus seems to have derived. As Copeland writes (2006, 392) "with hindsight, these theorems can be viewed as in effect a treatment of all the basic modal axioms and corresponding properties of the accessibility relation". Now in the work of Kanger and in the work of Montague the notion of relation used was that of a relation between models and not between possible worlds. The standard approach to the semantics of basic modal logic of nowadays was developed independently by various logicians between 1955 and 1959, notably by the work of Carew Meredith, Arthur Prior, Jaakko Hintikka and Saul Kripke. Jack Copeland (2006) gives the priority to the joint work of Meredith and Prior in 1956. In fact the work of Jaakko Hintikka and Saul Kripke was the better known version of the possible-world semantics. While the former delved in the epistemic reading of the box (to know) the second studied an ontological interpretation of the (Leibnizian) notion of necessity. Furthermore, in his early work Hintikka called the relation an *alternativeness* relation between possible states of affairs. In the context of deontic logic Hintikka (1957) calls the relation a

---

[18] Cf. Rahman 1997, 2000, Read 1999, Rahman/Redmond 2007.

copermissibility relation. Richard Montague initiated around 1975 a systematic application of modal languages for the formalization of natural language. Prior (1962) after a suggestion of Peter Geach (1960) called the relation "accessibility", which is now the standard name for the binary relation between possible worlds.[19] Hans Kamp extended the so-called Montague grammars to **Discourse Representation Theory** (DRT) which is nowadays the most influential paradigm to formalize natural language with application in various fields as, computer linguistics, artificial intelligence and philosophy. Through the work of Johan van Benthem; modal logic is understood as a formal language for the study of structures (Blackburn et alii 2002).

Contexts

The dialogical approach to modal logic requires a context-dependent notion of choice, that is to say, one in which the choices of the players are relative to different contexts in which the players perform their moves (attacks and defenses). The elements involved are

$$\boxed{\text{thesis + attacks + defenses + contexts}}$$

In a dialogue there is an initial context (represented by the level c_0) where the thesis has been uttered. As explained below, in the course of a dialogue other contexts such as c_1, $c_{1.1}$ $c_{1.2}$ $c_{1.1.1}$, etc., might occurr.

In the dialogical approach the meaning of the modal operator "$\Box$" is linked to the meaning of the utterance by a player X of the formula "$\Box A$" in a context c_0. And what does it mean to perform the utterance "$\Box A$" in the context c_0? Means that the individual X is committing itself to the utterance of A in any context available, chosen by the challenger Y from c_0. The choice of a context c_n by Y constitutes then an attack to which X responds by uttering A in c_n. Dually the meaning of "$\Diamond A$" involves the commitment of a player X (who utters $\Diamond A$) to the utterance of A in at least one context available of his own choice.

---

[19] cf. Copeland 2006, 384.

Similar as in the case of quantifiers, attacking or defending modal operators will concern choices. In the case of modal operators will concern choices of contexts. The choices of contexts are specified in the particle rules:

1. Particle Rules: box and diamond

Rule for the box

$\square$		
Formula uttered	Attack	Defense
$\square A[c_k]$	The attack is a question: ?	$A[c_i]$ A formula which must be defended: "!"
dialogical expressions:		
$N_1 = X\text{-}!\text{-}\square A[c_k]$	$N_2 = Y\text{-}?\text{-}\square[c_i]$ <u>Y has the choice</u> of the context, in this case is $[c_i]$	$N_3 = X\text{-}!\text{-} A[c_i]$ **X** must perform the defense in the context chosen by **Y**.
Explanation **X** utters the formula $\square A$ at the context $[c_k]$ and must be defended (!) Upon uttering $\square A$, the player **X** commits itself to uttering A in **any** context. How does **Y** challenge the utterance "$\square A[c_k]$"? Response: By demanding the utterance of A. Since **X** commits itself to the utterance of A in any context, then the challenger **Y** has the right to choose the context in which the utterance must be perform. Thus, the defense consists on uttering A within the context c_i chosen by **Y**.		

Rule for the diamond

$\lozenge$		
Formula uttered	Attack	Defense

$\Diamond A[c_k]$	The attack is a question: ?	$A[c_i]$
		A formula which must be defended: "!"

dialogical expressions:

$P_1=X\text{-!-}\Diamond A[c_k]$	$P_2=Y\text{-?-}\Diamond$	$P_3=X\text{-!-}A[c_i]$
		X has the choice of the context, in this case was $[c_i]$

Explanation

X utters the formula $\Diamond A$ at the context $[c_k]$ and must be defended (!) Upon uttering $\Diamond A$, the player **X** commits itself to uttering A in **at least one** context of his own choice. How does **Y** challenge the utterance "$\Diamond A[c_k]$"? Response: By demanding the utterance of A. Since **X** commits itself to the utterance of A in at least one context, then the challenger **Y** gives to **X** the choice of the context. Thus, the defense consists on uttering A within the context chosen by **X**.

Choices and Contexts

The choice of contexts – new or not new – is performed in the following cases:	➜	Attacking a box Defending a diamond

Introducing a context

To introduce a context means to choose a new one when attacking a box or defending a diamond. Indeed to choose a new one means to bring up a new context that was not previously included in the dialogue.

Box & diamond and the strategy of the players

One of the most important clauses to take into account is that the proponent never introduces contexts in a dialogue (with one exception explained below, namely the case of the logic D):

Box

If X utters □A, then Y has the choice of the context. But which context?

- If **P** utters □A, then **O** introduces always a new context.
- If **O** utters □A, then **P** chooses only a context already introduce by **O**.

Diamond

If X utters ◊A, then X has the choice of the context. But which context?

- If **O** utters ◊A, then **O** introduces always a new context.
- If **P** utters ◊A, then **P** chooses only a context already introduce by **O**.

Contexts and Index

To clarify the relationship between contexts and the choice of players, we introduced a system of indexation as well as a few definitions:

(i) There is a **departure context** (where the thesis was uttered) carrying the index 0 (c_0)

(ii) There are **levels**: The first context which is introduced from the context n (level 0) is noted n.1 (level 1), the second n.2 (level 1), etc. From n.1 (level 1): n.1.1 (level 2) and so on.

(iii) There is an **order relation**: "n>n.m" means that n is superior to n.m or n.m inferior to n.

(iv) **Depth of contexts**: Respect of n.m.l, we say that n is a *superior* context and of *depth 2*, conversely: Respect of n, we say that n.m.l is an *inferior* context and of *depth 2*.

Examples:

$c_{0.1}$ and $c_{0.2}$ are contexts chosen from c_0
 Both are inferior in one level in depth respect to c_0.

$c_{0.1.1}$ and $c_{0.1.2}$ are contexts chosen from $c_{0.1}$
 Both are inferior in one level in depth respect to $c_{0.1}$ and inferior in two levels in depth respect to c_0

Warning: at choosing contexts of *superior* or *inferior* level in depth, players must in principle follow the ordre of indexation. In other words, if not specified by extra rules (see Modal Dialogues and Configurations) from c_0 a player can choose $c_{0.1}$ or $c_{0.2}$ or choose $c_{0.1.1}$ or $c_{0.1.2}$ from $c_{0.1}$.

2. Structural rules

The aim of the structural rules is to provide a method of decision. What is at stake in a dialogue is to decide if there is a *wining strategy* for the thesis or not. Different structural rules will provide different methods of decision which caracterise different logics. As we did between classical amd intuitionistic logic, below we present the rules that diferenciate and caracterise logics **K, T, D, KB, K5, K4,** and **S4**, and the characteristic formulas representing each one of them.

Since in modal logic, all the moves are perfomed in contexts, it is necessary to replace the rule "(**SR-3**) (*Formal use of atomic formulas*)[20]" for the following:

(**SR-3-Modal Logic**) (*Formal use of atomic formulas in contexts*)
Atomic formulas can be uttered *for the first time* only by **O**. The proponent **P** can play an atomic formula only if the same formula was already uttered by **O** and in the <u>same context</u>. In other words: **P** can utter an atomic formula in a context c_i only if the same atomic formula was already granted in the same context c_i by **O**. Atomic formulas cannot be attacked.

Logic K

Structural Rules for logic K:
1. (**SR-3-Modal Logic**)
2. (**SR-K**): **P** can only choose contexts (levels) introduced before by O.

We say that $\Box(A\rightarrow B)\rightarrow(\Box A\rightarrow\Box B)$ characterizes logic K, because it has a winning strategy if and only if the structural rules are the followings: (**SR-3-Modal Logic**) and (**SR-K**).

---

[20] See "12.2 Rules"

The contexts (levels) are indicated in the columns signalised by c.

c	O			P		c
				$\Box(A{\to}B){\to}(\Box A{\to}\Box B)$	0	c_0
c_0	1	$\Box(A{\to}B)$	0	$\Box A{\to}\Box B$	2	c_0
c_0	3	$\Box A$	2	$\Box B$	4	c_0
c_0	5	$?\text{-}\Box c_{0.1}$	4	B ☺	12	$c_{0.1}$
$c_{0.1}$	7	A	3	$?\text{-}\Box c_{0.1}$	6	c_0
$c_{0.1}$	9	$A{\to}B$	1	$?\text{-}\Box c_{0.1}$	8	c_0
$c_{0.1}$	11	B	9	A	10	$c_{0.1}$

Note: In the following, the difference between logics T, KB, K5, K4, and S4 is established by the structural rule that governs the choice of contexts when attacking a box or defending a diamond.

Logic T

Structural Rules for logic T:

1. (**SR-3-Modal Logic**)
2. (**SR-K**): **P** can only choose contexts (levels) introduced before by **O**.
3. (**SR-T**): If **P** is at the context c_i, **P** may choose the context c_i when defending a diamond or attacking a box.

We say that $\Box A{\to}A$ characterizes logic T, because it has a winning strategy if and only if the structural rules are the followings: (**SR-3-Modal Logic**), (**SR-K**) and (**SR-T**).

c	O			P		c
				$\Box A{\to}A$	0	c_0
c_0	1	$\Box A$	0			

A dialogue without (**SR-T**) stops here. But if we play with (**SR-T**), the proponent can move further and win:

c	O				P		c
					□A→A	0	c_0
c_0	1	□A	0		A☺	4	c_0
c_0	3	A		1	?-□c_0	2	c_0

In move 2 the proponent could can the same context (departure level) when attacking a box.

Logic KB

Structural Rules for logic KB:
1. (**SR-3-Modal Logic**)
2. (**SR-K**): **P** can only choose contexts (levels) introduced before by O.
3. (**SR-KB**): After the choice of a new context, **P** can choose any superior in dexed context.

We say that A→□◊A characterizes logic KB because it has a winning strategy if and only if the structural rules are the followings: (**SR-3-Modal Logic**), (**SR-K**) and (**SR-KB**).

c	O				P		c
					A→□◊A	0	c_0
c_0	1	A	0		□◊A	2	c_0
c_0	3	?-□ $c_{0.1}$	2		◊A	4	$c_{0.1}$
$c_{0.1}$	5	?◊	4		A ☺	6	c_0

In move 6 the proponent chooses a *superior* indexed context (0>0.1)

Logic K5

Structural Rules for logic K5:
1. (**SR-3-Modal Logic**)
2. (**SR-K**): **P** can only choose contexts (levels) introduced before by O.
3. (**SR-K5**): After the choice of two news contexts indexed n.m and n.(m+i) (i≠0), **P** can choose any context of the same depth. In other words, if we assume that **O** has already introduced $c_{n.m}$ and $c_{n.k}$. If **P** is at

$c_{n.m}$ he may choose $c_{n.k}$ and viceversa: if **P** is at $c_{n.k}$ he may choose $c_{n.m}$.

We say that $\Diamond A \rightarrow \Box \Diamond A$ characterizes logic K5 because it has a winning strategy if and only if the structural rules are the followings: (**SR-3-Modal Logic**), (**SR-K**) and (**SR-K5**).

c		O			P		c
					$\Diamond A \rightarrow \Box \Diamond A$	0	c_0
c_0	1	$\Diamond A$	0		$\Box \Diamond A$	2	c_0
c_0	3	?-$\Box c_{0.1}$	2		$\Diamond A$	4	$c_{0.1}$
$c_{0.1}$	5	?$\Diamond$	4		A ☺	8	$c_{0.2}$
$c_{0.2}$	7	A		1	?$\Diamond$	6	c_0

In move 8, **P** chooses a context of the same level (level 1)

Logic K4

Structural Rules for logic K4:
1. (**SR-3-Modal Logic**)
2. (**SR-K**): **P** can only choose contexts (levels) introduced before by O.
3. (**SR-K4**): **P** can choose any inferior two levels in depth context.

We say that $\Box A \rightarrow \Box \Box A$ characterizes logic K4 because it has a winning strategy if and only if the structural rules are the followings: (**SR-3-Modal Logic**), (**SR-K**) and (**SR-K4**).

c		O			P		c
					$\Box A \rightarrow \Box \Box A$	0	c_0
c_0	1	$\Box A$	0		$\Box \Box A$	2	c_0
c_0	3	?-$\Box c_{0.1}$	2		$\Box A$	4	$c_{0.1}$
c_1	5	?-$\Box c_{0.1.1}$	4		A ☺	8	$c_{0.1.1}$
$c_{0.1.1}$	7	A		1	?-$\Box c_{0.1.1}$	6	c_0

In move 6, **P** attacks by choosing an inferior two levels in depth context.

Logic S4

Structural Rules for logic S4:
1. **(SR-3-Modal Logic)**
2. **(SR-K)**: P can only choose contexts (levels) introduced before by O.
3. **(SR-K4)**: P can choose any inferior two levels in depth context.
4. **(SR-T)**: P can choose the same context (level) when defending a diamond or attacking a box.

We say that $\Box A \rightarrow \Diamond\Box\Diamond\Box\Diamond A$ characterizes logic S4 because it has a winning strategy if and only if the structural rules are the followings: **(SR-3-Modal Logic)**, **(SR-K)**, **(SR-K4)** and **(SR-T)**.

c	O				P		c
					$\Box A \rightarrow \Diamond\Box\Diamond\Box\Diamond A$	0	c_0
c_0	1	$\Box A$	0		$\Diamond\Box\Diamond\Box\Diamond A$	2	c_0
c_0	3	$?\Diamond$	2		$\Box\Diamond\Box\Diamond A$	4	c_0
c_0	5	$?\text{-}\Box c_{0.1}$	4		$\Diamond\Box\Diamond A$	6	$c_{0.1}$
$c_{0.1}$	7	$?\Diamond$	6		$\Box\Diamond A$	8	$c_{0.1}$
$c_{0.1}$	9	$?\text{-}\Box c_{0.1.1}$	8		$\Diamond A$	10	$c_{0.1.1}$
$c_{0.1.1}$	11	$?\Diamond$	10		A ☺	14	$c_{0.1.1}$
$c_{0.1.1}$	13	A		1	$?\text{-}\Box c_{0.1.1}$	12	c_0

In move 12 we play with **(SR-K4)** and in move 14 with **(SR-T)**

In the following case, logic D, **P can introduce contexts** and we lost rule **(SR-K)**.

Logic D

Structural Rules for logic D:
1. **(SR-3-Modal Logic)**

3. **(SR-D)**: P can choose any *inferior* indexed context.[21] In other words, if we assume that P is at c_0, P may choose a contex $c_{0.1}$ though it has not been introduced by O before.

We say that $\Box A \rightarrow \Diamond A$ characterizes logic D, because it has a winning strategy if and only if the structural rules are the followings: **(SR-3-Modal Logic)** and **(SR-D)**.

c	O			P		c
				$\Box A \rightarrow \Diamond A$	0	c_0
c_0	1	$\Box A$	0	$\Diamond A$	2	c_0
c_0	3	$?\Diamond$	2	A ☺	6	$c_{0.1}$
$c_{0.1}$	5	A		1	$?\text{-}\Box c_{0.1}$	4	c_0

In move 6, P introduces a context by choosing an *inferior* indexed one (0>0.1).

Summary

Logic **K**: (SR-3-Modal Logic) + (SR-K): P can choose contexts (levels) that O has chosen before.

Logics **T, KB, K5, K4**, and **S4**: (SR-3-Modal Logic) + (SR-K) + (SR-T, SR-KB, SR-K5, SR-K4, SR-S4 respectively)

Logic **D**: (SR-3-Modal Logic) + ~~(SR-K)~~ + (SR-D)

In the following we present some exercises in logic K:

---

[21] See "(iv) Depth of contexts" in "Contexts and Index"

Exercises

Case 41: D($\square$(p→p)) in logic K

c_0 =departure context

c		O			P		c
					$\square$(p→p)	0	c_0
c_0	1	?-$\square c_{0.1}$	0		(p→p)	2	$c_{0.1}$
$c_{0.1}$	3	p	2		p ☺	4	$c_{0.1}$

Move 0: $N_1=<\tau$, P-!-$\square$(p→p)>	The utterance of **P** is in the context c_0
Move 1: $N_2=<$ **CH**, O-?-$\square c_{0.1}$>	O introduces a new context: $c_{0.1}$
Move 2: $I_3=<$**D**, P-!-(p→p)>	**P** must utter p→p in $c_{0.1}$ A new play equivalent to I_1 for X=P starts here.
Move 3: $I_2=<$**CH**, O-!-p>	
Move 4: $I_3=<$**D**, P-!-p>	☺
Score **P wins** by making the last move: the dialogue is *finished* and *closed*, O can not move further, and the same atomic formula appears in the last two moves: 3 and 4.	

Case 42: D($\lozenge$p→p) in logic K

c		O				P		c
						$\lozenge$p→p	0	c_0
c_0	1	$\lozenge$p	0					
$c_{0.1}$	3	p ☺			1	?-$\lozenge$	2	c_0

Move 0: $I_1=<\tau,$ P-!-$\Diamond$p$\rightarrow$p>	The utterance of **P** is in the context c_0
Move 1: $I_2=<$ **CH**, O-!-$\Diamond$p>	The defense corresponding to this attack must be performed in the context c_0 A new play equivalent to P_1 for X=**P** starts here
Move 2: $P_2=<$ **CH**, P-?-$\Diamond$>	
Move 3: $P_3=<D,$ O-!-p>	To prevent **P** from taking advantage of the defence, **O** introduces a new context: $c_{0.1}$
Score **O wins** by making the last move: the dialogue is *finished* and *open,* **P** can not move further, and no two positions feature the same atomic formula.	

Case 43: D(p→□p) in logic K

c		O				P		c
						p→□p	0	c_0
c_0	1	p	0			□p	2	c_0
c_0	3	?-□$c_{0.1}$ ☺	2					

Move 0: $I_1=<\tau,$ P-!- p$\rightarrow$□p>	The utterance of **P** is in the context c_0
Move 1: $I_2=<$ **CH**, O-!-p>	
Move 2: $I_3=<D,$ P-!-□p >	A new play equivalent to N_1 for X=**P** starts here
Move 3: $N_2=<$ **CH**, O-?-□$c_{0.1}$>	The defence corresponding to this attack must be performed in the context c_0 To prevent **P** from taking advantage of the defence, **O** introduces a new context: $c_{0.1}$
Score **O wins** by making the last move:	

> the dialogue is *finished* and *open*,
> **P** can not move further, and no two positions feature the same atomic formula.

Case 44: D($\square p \rightarrow \square p$) in logic K

c		O			P		c
					$\square p \rightarrow \square p$	0	c_0
c_0	1	$\square p$	0		$\square p$	2	c_0
c_0	3	?-$\square c_{0.1}$	2		p ☺	6	c_1
$c_{0.1}$	5	p		1	?-$\square c_{0.1}$	4	c_0

Move 0: I_1=<τ, **P**-!- $\square p \rightarrow \square p$>	The utterance of **P** is in the context c_0
Move 1: I_2=< **CH**, **O**-!-$\square p$>	A new play equivalent to N_1 for X=**O** starts here
Move 2: I_3=<**D**, **P**-!-$\square p$ >	A new play equivalent to N_1 for X=**P** starts here
Move 3: N_2=< **CH**, **O**-?-$\square c_{0.1}$>	The defence corresponding to this attack must be performed in the new context $c_{0.1}$ introduced by **O**
Move 4: N_2=< **CH**, **P**-?-$\square c_{0.1}$>	**P** chooses the same context $c_{0.1}$ to take advantage of the previous defence by **O**
Move 5: N_3=<**D**, **O**-!-p >	
Move 6: N_3=<**D**, **P**-!-p >	

Score
P wins by making the last move:
the dialogue is *finished* and *closed*,
O can not move further, and the same atomic
formula appears in the last two moves: 5 and 6.

Case 45: $D(\Diamond p \to \Box p)$ in logic K

c	O			P			c
					$\Diamond p \to \Box p$	0	c_0
c_0	1	$\Diamond p$	0		$\Box p$	2	c_0
c_0	3	?-$\Box c_{0.1}$	2				
$c_{0.2}$	5	p ☺		1	?-$\Diamond$	4	c_0

Move 0: $I_1 = \langle \tau,\ \text{P-!-}\ \Diamond p \to \Box p\rangle$	**P** utters the formula $\Diamond p \to \Box p$ in the context c_0
Move 1: $I_2 = \langle\ CH,\ \text{O-!-}\Diamond p\rangle$	A new play equivalent to P_1 for $X=O$ starts here
Move 2: $I_3 = \langle D,\ \text{P-!-}\Box p\ \rangle$	A new play equivalent to N_1 for $X=P$ starts here
Move 3: $N_2 = \langle\ CH,\ \text{O-?-}\Box c_{0.1}\rangle$	The defence corresponding to this attack must be performed in the new context $c_{0.1}$ chosen by O
Move 4: $P_2 = \langle\ CH,\ \text{P-?-}\Diamond\ \rangle$	
Move 5: $P_3 = \langle D,\ \text{O-!-}p\ \rangle$	O introduces a new context ($c_{0.2}$) preventing P from obtaining "p" in the context c_0
Score	

Score

O wins by making the last move:
the dialogue is *finished* and *open,*
P can not move further, and no two positions feature the same atomic formula.

Case 46: $D(\Diamond p \to \Diamond p)$ in logic K

c	O			P		c
				$\Diamond p \to \Diamond p$	0	c_0
c_0	1	$\Diamond p$	0	$\Diamond p$	2	c_0
c_0	3	?-$\Diamond$	2	p ☺	6	$c_{0.1}$
$c_{0.1}$	5	p		1	?-$\Diamond$	4	c_0

Move 0: $I_1 = \langle \tau, \text{P-!- } \Diamond p \to \Diamond p \rangle$	The utterance of **P** is in the context c_0
Move 1: $I_2 = \langle \textbf{\textit{CH}}, \text{O-!-}\Diamond p \rangle$	A new play equivalent to P_1 for X=**O** starts here
Move 2: $I_3 = \langle \textbf{\textit{D}}, \text{P-!-}\Diamond p \rangle$	A new play equivalent to P_1 for X=**P** starts here
Move 3: $P_2 = \langle \textbf{\textit{CH}}, \text{O-?-}\Diamond \rangle$	
Move 4: $P_2 = \langle \textbf{\textit{CH}}, \text{P-?-}\Diamond \rangle$	
Move 5: $P_3 = \langle \textbf{\textit{D}}, \text{O-!-p} \rangle$	O introduces the new context $c_{0.1}$
Move 6: $P_3 = \langle \textbf{\textit{D}}, \text{O-!-p} \rangle$	P takes advantage of the last move

Score
P wins by making the last move:
the dialogue is *finished* and *closed,*
O can not move further, and the same atomic
formula appears in the last two moves: 5 and 6.

We leave the explanations of the two following exercises to the reader:

Case 47: D($\Box$(p→q)→($\Box$p→$\Box$q)) in logic K

c		O			P		c
					$\Box$(p→q)→($\Box$p→$\Box$q)	0	c_0
c_0	1	$\Box$(p→q)	0		$\Box$p→$\Box$q	2	c_0
c_0	3	$\Box$p	2		$\Box$q	4	c_0
c_0	5	?-$\Box c_{0.1}$	4		q ☺	12	$c_{0.1}$
$c_{0.1}$	7	p→q		1	?-$\Box c_{0.1}$	6	c_0
$c_{0.1}$	9	p		3	?-$\Box c_{0.1}$	8	c_0
$c_{0.1}$	11	q		7	p	10	$c_{0.1}$

Case 48: D(($\Box$p∧$\Box$q)→$\Box$(p∧q)) in logic K

c		O			P		c
					($\Box$p→$\Box$q)→$\Box$(p∧q)	0	c_0
c_0	1	($\Box$p∧$\Box$q)	0		$\Box$(p∧q)	2	c_0
c_0	3	?-$\Box c_{0.1}$	2		p∧q	4	$c_{0.1}$
$c_{0.1}$	5	?-$\wedge_1$	4		p	12	$c_{0.1}$
c_0	7	$\Box$p		1	?-$\wedge_1$	6	$c_{0.1}$
c_0	9	$\Box$q		1	?-$\wedge_2$	8	$c_{0.1}$
$c_{0.1}$	11	p		7	?-$\Box c_{0.1}$	10	c_0
$c_{0.1}$	13	?-$\wedge_2$	4		q ☺	16	$c_{0.1}$
$c_{0.1}$	15	q		9	?-$\Box c_{0.1}$	14	c_0

Dialogical Logic and Possible-Worlds Semantics

Just for the sake of illustration, we can establish a correspondence between the dialogues for modal propositional logic and Kripke's possible worlds semantics.

A Semantics for Modal Logic

A semantics for modal logic is built upon the concepts of *frame* and *model* [22].

A frame is a couple F= <W, R>, where W is a non empty set and R a binary relation on the set W, i.e., a subset of the set WxW. The set W is called the "universe", the elements of W = "possible worlds" and R="accessibility relation". Thus, a frame consists of a set W of possible worlds connected by an *accessibility* relation R. Consider two worlds w_0 and w_1 belonging to the universe W, $w_0 R w_1$ means that w_1 is accessible from the world w_0.

A model consists of a triple M=<W, R, V> built from a frame <W, R> and the function V. Let P be the set of propositions of our language L, V is an application that associates to each proposition of P a subset V(p) of W. In other words, V(p) is the set of elements of W (possible worlds) where the proposition p is true.

For the modal operators, according to a formulation attributed to Leibniz, a proposition (p) is *necessarily* true ($\Box p$) if it is verified in all possible worlds; while a proposition (p) is *possibly* true ($\Diamond p$) if it is verified in at least one possible world.

Formally:
$\Box p$ is true in wi $\in$ M if and only if p is true in all possible worlds wj verifying wiRwj. [In other words: p is necessary true in the world wi belonging to the model M, if and only if p is true in all possible worlds wj accessible from wi.]

---

[22] With this purpose, we follow in general terms the book of Gochet & Gribomont &Thayse, Vol. 3 (2000).

◊p is true in wi ∈ M if and only if p is true in at least one possible worlds wj verifying wiRwj. [In other words: p is possibly true in the world wi belonging to the model M, if and only if p is true in at least one possible world wj accessible from wi.]

Model, Frame and Validity

<u>Definition of validity in a model</u>: A formula φ is valid in a model if φ is true in all the worlds of the model.
<u>Definition of validity in a frame</u>: A formula φ is valid in a frame if φ is valid in all models built from this frame.
<u>Definition of validity</u>: A formula φ is valid if φ is valid in all frames.

Intuitively, we can represent a set of possible worlds and their accessibility relations with points and arrows between them, respectively. For example, for the set $W = \{w_0, w_1, w_2\}$, and the accessibility relations w_0Rw_1, w_1Rw_0 and w_1Rw_2 we have:

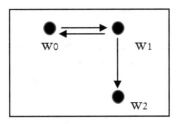

Dialogues and Possible World Semantics

How do dialogues and possible world semantics relate? Well, in the resolution of a dialogue, from a strategic point of view, **O** is trying to build a counter-model against the thesis uttered by **P**. For **P** to have a winning strategy for the thesis means that **O** failed at building a counter model and thus the thesis is valid. **O** builds a counter model by introducing possible worlds and accessibility relations. Let's see that in more detail.

Necessity, Possibility and the Strategy of Players

The notions we have are:

(i) Possible worlds (w_0, w_1, w_2, ...)= Contexts (c_1, $c_{1.1}$ $c_{1.2}$ $c_{1.1.1}$, ...)

(ii) Accessibility relations R

We remember that:

Players build a new accessibility relation by introducing a new or not new possible world:	➜	By attacking a box or By defending a diamond

Let's see now when and how they are built:

Item 1: Necessity ($\square$)

If **X** utters $\square A$, then **Y** has the choice of the possible world (see "Box & diamond and the strategy of the players"). But which possible world?

Item 1.1: If **P** utters $\square A$, **O** always chooses a new possible world introducing a new accessibility relation.

Item 1.2: If **O** utters $\square A$, **P** can choose possible worlds through accessibility relations already introduced by **O**. In other words: **P** can choose only possible worlds for which the accessibility relation has already been built by **O**.

Item 2: Possibility ($\lozenge$)

If **X** utters $\lozenge A$, then **X** has the choice of the possible world. (see "Box & diamond and the strategy of the players"). But which possible world?

Item 2.1: If **O** utters $\lozenge A$, **O** chooses always a new possible world introducing a new accessibility relation. In other words: **O** defends itself always introducing a new relation of accessibility to a new world.

Item 2.2: If **P** utters $\lozenge A$, **P** can choose possible worlds through accessibility relations already introduced by **O**. In other words: **P** can choose only possible worlds for which the accessibility relation has already been built by **O**.

Item 3:

P never introduces a new relation of accessibility, save but under logic D.

Let's see now some exercises. For the sake of clarity, it is the repetition of precedent cases.

Exercises for Possible Worlds Semantics

Case 49: $D(\Box(p\rightarrow p))$ in logic K

(Repetition of case 41)

w	O			P		w
				$\Box(p\rightarrow p)$	0	w_0
w_0	1	?-$\Box w_1$	0	$(p\rightarrow p)$	2	w_1
w_1	3	p	2	p ☺	4	w_1

Description of Moves	Building of Accessibility Relations
Move 0: $N_1=<\tau,$ P-!-$\Box(p\rightarrow p)>$	The utterance of **P** is in the possible world w_0 ● w_0
Move 1: $N_2=<$ *CH,* O-?-$\Box w_1>$	O introduces the accessibility relation $w_0 R w_1$ to the new possible world w_1 (see Item 1.1) $\quad$ w_0 ● → ● w_1
Move 2: $I_3=<D,$ P-!-$(p\rightarrow p)>$	**P** must utter $p\rightarrow p$ in w_1. (see Item 3) A new play equivalent to I_1 for X=**P** starts here
Move 3: $I_2=<$ *CH,* O-!-p>	O utters "p" in w_1
Move 4: $I_3=<D,$ P-!-p>	**P** takes advantage of move 3 ☺
Score **P** wins because s/he did the last move, the dialogue is finished, i.e. **O** can not further move,	

and closed, i.e. the same atomic formula appears in moves 3 and 4.

Case 50: $D(\Diamond p \rightarrow p)$ in logic K

(Repetition of case 42)

w		O			P		w
					$\Diamond p \rightarrow p$	0	w_0
w_0	1	$\Diamond p$	0				
w_1	3	p ☺		1	?-$\Diamond$	2	w_0

Description of Moves	Building of accessibility relations
Move 0: $I_1 = <\tau, \text{P-!-}\Diamond p \rightarrow p>$	The utterance of **P** is in the possible world w_0 ● w_0
Move 1: $I_2 = < \boldsymbol{CH}, \text{O-!-}\Diamond p>$	The defence corresponding to this attack must be performed in w_0 A new play equivalent to P_1 for X=P starts here
Move 2: $P_2 = < \boldsymbol{CH}, \text{P-?-}\Diamond>$	
Move 3: $P_3 = <\boldsymbol{D}, \text{O-!-}p>$	To prevent **P** from taking advantage of the defence, **O** introduces a new possible world (w_1), building at once an accessibility relation (see Item 2.1): w_0 ● →● w_1

Score
O wins because s/he did the last move,
the dialogue is *finished*: **P** can not further move
and *open*: no atomic formula appears in two positions.

Case 51: $D(\Diamond p \to \Box p)$ in logic K

(Repetition of case 45)

w		O			P		w
					$\Diamond p \to \Box p$	0	w_0
w_0	1	$\Diamond p$	0		$\Box p$	2	w_0
w_0	3	?-$\Box w_1$	2				
w_2	5	p ☺		1	?-$\Diamond$	4	w_0

Description of Moves	Building of accessibility relations
Move 0: $I_1 = <\tau, P\text{-!-}\Diamond p \to \Box p>$	The utterance of **P** is in the possible world w_0 ● w_0
Move 1: $I_2 = < \textbf{\textit{CH}}, O\text{-!-}\Diamond p>$	A new play equivalent to P_1 for X=O starts here
Move 2: $I_3 = <\textbf{\textit{D}}, P\text{-!-}\Box p >$	A new play equivalent to N_1 for X=P starts here
Move 3: $N_2 = < \textbf{\textit{CH}}, O\text{-?-}\Box w_1>$	**O** introduces an accessibility relation to w_1. The defence corresponding to this attack must be performed in this new possible world introduced by **O** (w_1) (see Item 1.1) w_0 ● → ● w_1
Move 4: $P_2 = < \textbf{\textit{CH}}, P\text{-?-}\Diamond>$	
Move 5: $P_3 = <\textbf{\textit{D}}, O\text{-!-}p >$	To prevent **P** from taking advantage of the defence, **O** introduces a new possible world (w_2), building the new accessibility relation $w_0 R w_1$ from w_0 (see Item 2.1) w_0 ● → ● w_1 ↓ ● w_2
Score O wins because s/he did the last move, the dialogue is *finished*: **P** can not further move	

and *open*: no two positions feature the same atomic formula.

Case 52: D(□p→□p) in logic K

(A variant of case 45)

w		O			P		w
					□p→□p	0	w_0
w_0	1	□p	0		□p	2	w_0
w_0	3	?-□w_1	2		p ☺		w_1
w_1	5	p		1	?-□w_1	4	w_0

Upon performing the attack of move 4, **P** takes advantage of the accessibility relation w_0Rw_1 already introduced by **O** when performing the move 3 (see Item 1.2). In the next variant of the case, **P** does not have this possibility:

Case 53: D(□p→◊p) in logic K

(Another variant of case 45)

w		O			P		w
					□p→◊p	0	w_0
w_0	1	□p	0		◊p	2	w_0
w_0	3	?-◊	2				
		☺			?-□X	4	w_0

P can not perform the attack of move 4 because there is no accessibility relation already introduced by **O**.

K, T, KB, K5, K4, D AND POSSIBLE WORLD SEMANTICS

K, T, KB, K5, K4 and D are frames characterised by their having *conditions*. We define a *system* as the set of all the frames having the same condition. The most important conditions are:

- Reflexivity: {wi$R$wi}
- Symmetry: {wi$R$wj and wj$R$wi}
- Transitivity: {wi$R$wj, wj$R$wk and wi$R$wk}
- Seriality: {for every world wi there is some world wj such that wi$R$wj}[23]

All the frames corresponding to the same system are characterized (or identified) as having a dialogically winning strategy for certain formulas. Thus, a frame is characterized as belonging to a particular system, if and only if there is a winning strategy in that frame for a specific formula. There is a sense in which any such formula expresses a property of the configuration.

System K

–There are no conditions on the frame –

We say that $\Box(A{\rightarrow}B){\rightarrow}(\Box A{\rightarrow}\Box B)$ characterizes system K because it has a winning strategy if and only if we do not need any condition on the frame.

w		O				P		w
					$\Box(A{\rightarrow}B){\rightarrow}(\Box A{\rightarrow}\Box B)$	0	w$_0$
w$_0$	1	$\Box(A{\rightarrow}B)$	0		$\Box A{\rightarrow}\Box B$	2	w$_0$
w$_0$	3	$\Box A$	2		$\Box B$	4	w$_0$
w$_0$	5	?-$\Box$w$_1$	4		B ☺	12	w$_1$
w$_1$	7	A		3	?-$\Box$w$_1$	6	w$_0$
w$_1$	9	A$\rightarrow$B		1	?-$\Box$w$_1$	8	w$_0$
w$_1$	11	B		9	A	10	w$_1$

---

[23] From a temporal point of view it means that there is no last moment in time.

System T

– The condition that characterizes System T is Reflexivity –

We say that $\Box A \rightarrow A$ characterizes reflexivity because it has a winning strategy if and only if the frame is reflexive. From a dialogical point of view, reflexivity is a concession made for the Opponent.

w	O			P			w
	Concession: w_0Rw_0			$\Box A \rightarrow A$		0	w_0
w_0	1	$\Box A$	0		A ☺	4	w_0
w_0	3	A		1	$?\text{-}\Box w_0$	2	w_0

P can win the dialogue only if every context is accessible from itself.

Intuitively, a minimal case will correspond to the following, which is a condition on the frame and not an accessibility relation introduced by O.	↪● w_0

System D

– The condition that characterizes System D is Seriality –

We say that $\Box A \rightarrow \Diamond A$ characterizes seriality because it has a winning strategy if and only if the frame is serial. From a dialogical point of view, seriality is a concession made for the Opponent.

w	O			P			w
	Concession: Seriality			$\Box A \rightarrow \Diamond A$		0	w_0
w_0	1	$\Box A$	0		$\Diamond A$	2	w_0
w_0	3	$?\Diamond$	2		A ☺	6	w_1
w_1	5	A		1	$?\text{-}\Box w_1$	4	w_0

The formula is valid if and only if, whatever the context, P can always introduce a new relation of accessibility to a new possible world.

Intuitively, a minimal case will correspond to the following, which is a condition on the frame and not an accessibility relation introduced by O.	$w_0 \bullet \rightarrow \bullet\ w_1$

System KB

– The condition that characterizes system KB is Symmetry–

We say that $A \rightarrow \Box\Diamond A$ characterizes symmetry because it has a winning strategy if and only if the frame is symmetrical. From a dialogical point of view, symmetry is a concession made for the Opponent.

w	O			P		w
	Concession: when introducing wiRwj, concedes wjRwi			$A \rightarrow \Box\Diamond A$	0	w_0
w_0	1	A	0	$\Box\Diamond A$	2	w_0
w_0	3	?-$\Box w_1$	2	$\Diamond A$	4	w_1
w_1	5	?$\Diamond$	4	A ☺	6	w_0

P can win the dialogue only if the context w_0 is accessible since w_1

Intuitively, a minimal case will correspond to the following design. When O introduces w_0Rw_1 in move 3, it concedes at the same time w_1Rw_0 (which is a condition presupposed on the frame and not an accessibility relation introduced by O).	$w_0 \bullet \leftrightarrows \bullet\ w_1$

System K5

– Euclidean frames –

We say that $\Diamond A \rightarrow \Box\Diamond A$ characterizes system K5 because it has a winning strategy if and only if the frame is Euclidean. A frame is Euclidean if: When O introduces w_0Rw_1 and w_0Rw_2 is conceding at the same time w_2Rw_1 and w_1Rw_2

w		O				P		w
		Concession: w_2Rw_1 and w_1Rw_2				$\lozenge A \rightarrow \square \lozenge A$	0	w_0
w_0	1	$\lozenge A$	0			$\square \lozenge A$	2	w_0
w_0	3	$? \, w_1$	2			$\lozenge A$	4	w_1
w_1	5	$?\lozenge$	4			A ☺	8	w_2
w_2	7	A		1		$?\lozenge$	6	w_0

P can win the dialogue only if the context w_2 is accessible from w_1

Intuitively, a minimal case will correspond to the following design. When O introduces w_0Rw_1 in move 3 and w_0Rw_2 in move 7, it concedes at the same time w_2Rw_1 and w_1Rw_2 (which are conditions presupposed on the frame and not an accessibility relations introduced by O).

System K4

– The condition that characterizes System K4 is Transitivity –

We say that $\square A \rightarrow \square \square A$ characterizes transitivity because it has a winning strategy if and only if the frame is transitive. From a dialogical point of view, transitivity is a concession made for the Opponent.

w		O				P		w
		Concession: Transitivity				$\square A \rightarrow \square \square A$	0	w_0
w_0	1	$\square A$	0			$\square \square A$	2	w_0
w_0	3	$?\text{-}\square w_1$	2			$\square A$	4	w_1
w_1	5	$?\text{-}\square \, w_2$	4			A	8	w_2
w_2	7	A		1		$?\text{-}\square w_2$	6	w_0

P can win the dialogue only if the context w_2 is accessible since w_0

Intuitively, a minimal case will correspond to the following design. When **O** introduces w_0Rw_1 in move 3 and w_1Rw_2 in move 5, it concedes at the same time w_0Rw_2 (which is a condition presupposed on the frame and not an accessibility relation introduced by **O**).

System S4

– The conditions that characterize System S4 are Reflexivity and Transitivity

–

We say that $\Box A \rightarrow \Diamond\Box\Diamond\Box\Diamond A$ characterizes S4 because it has a winning strategy if and only if the frame is reflexive and transitive. From a dialogical point of view, reflexivity and transitivity are concessions made for the Opponent.

w		O			P		w
					$\Box A \rightarrow \Diamond\Box\Diamond\Box\Diamond A$	0	w_0
w_0	1	$\Box A$	0		$\Diamond\Box\Diamond\Box\Diamond A$	2	w_0
w_0	3	$?\Diamond$	2		$\Box\Diamond\Box\Diamond A$	4	w_0
w_0	5	$?\text{-}\Box w_1$	4		$\Diamond\Box\Diamond A$	6	w_1
w_1	7	$?\Diamond$	6		$\Box\Diamond A$	8	w_1
w_1	9	$?\text{-}\Box w_2$	8		$\Diamond A$	10	w_2
w_2	11	$?\Diamond$	10		A	14	w_2
w_2	13	A		1	$?\text{-}\Box w_2$	12	w_0

P can win the dialogue only if the context w_1 is accessible from itself and w_2 from w_0

Intuitively, a minimal case will correspond to the following design. When **O** introduces w_0Rw_1 in move 3 and w_1Rw_2 in move 5, it concedes at the same time w_0Rw_2 (which is a condition presupposed on the frame and not an accessibility relation introduced by **O**).

Appendix

On Branching

The notion of branching was introduced for the first time by Rahman and Keiff (2004) in the context of an overview on dialogical logic. The point was to explain briefly the relation between winning strategies and tableaux while describing the dialogical approach to validity.

Strictly speaking the type of branching deployed in our text is a feature of strategies not of the play level: from a strategic point of view the Proponent is not interested in producing branches (since then it is tougher to achieve his means) while the Opponent is. Indeed, the Opponent prefers to restrict the scope of the concessions of atomic formulas in such a way that they are conceded, for example, in one branch but not in the other. In the paper mentioned above, Rahman and Keiff called this branching /asymmetric/ branching.

A *symmetric* branching follows if we allow both players to branch the dialogue or not (even if it might come out that, branching was at a particular position of the game a wrong decision). Symmetric branching is the one that can be placed at the play level. However, in order to stress the play level and to work out those features that distinguish dialogues from the other approaches (such as semantic tableaux) one can totally avoid th use of branching rules.

In the present text we introduced **asymmetric** branching as a structural rule in order to facilitate to the layman the use of dialogues in the context of proving validity. However it is crucial to recall that conceptually speaking asymmetric branching is not part of the play level.

Authors

Juan Redmond wrote his PhD dissertation, entitled *Dynamic Logic of Fiction. For a dialogical approach* (Lille 2010), under the supervision of Prof. Shahid Rahman at the University of Lille 3. Redmond is currently an associated member of the laboratory *Savoirs, Textes, Langage* (UMR8163) and an active collaborator of the research group *Pragmatisme Dialogique* headed by Shahid Rahman (Lille 3).

Main Publications: [2007]: « Hugh McColl and the birth of logical pluralism» (with Shahid Rahman), D.Gabbay/J.Woods, ***Handbook of the history of logic***, vol.4, **Elsevier**. p.536-606; [2007]: *Hugh MacColl. An overview of his Logical Work with Anthology* (with Shahid Rahman), College Publications; [2007]: Translation of the book *Gottlob Frege zur Einführung* by Markus Stepanians, College Publications ("Cuadernos de Lógica, Epistemología y Lenguaje", vol.1); [2008]: *Logique Dialogique : une introduction – Première partie : Méthode de dialogique : règles et exercices* (with Matthieu Fontaine), col. Cahiers de logique et d'épistémologie, Vol. 5, D. Gabbay & Sh. Rahman Eds., College Publications, London; [2008]: *Hugh MacColl et la naissance du pluralisme logique* (with Shahid Rahman), in "Cahiers de logique et Épistémologie" N°3, College Publications.; [2011]: *Logique dynamique de la fiction: pour une approche dialogique*, in "Cahiers de logique et Epistémologie", D. Gabbay & Sh. Rahman Eds., College Publications, London. (in print); [2011]: "To Be is To Be Chosen – A Dialogical Understanding of Ontological Commitment" (with Matthieu Fontaine), in *Logic of Knowledge. Theory and Applications*, C. Bares Gomez, S. Magniez et F. Salguero (eds.), col. Dialogues and Games of Logic, Sh. Rahman, N. Clerbout et M. Fontaine (eds.), College Publication, London (submitted).

juanredmond@yahoo.fr

Matthieu Fontaine is a PhD student under the supervision of Prof. Shahid Rahman at the University of Lille 3. Fontaine is currently writing his dissertation on intentional objects He is currently an associated member of the laboratory *Savoirs, Textes, Langage* (UMR8163) and an active collaborator of the research group *Pragmatisme Dialogique* headed by Shahid Rahman (Lille 3).

Main Publications: [2012]: "Individuality in Fiction and the Creative Role of the Reader" (with Shahid Rahman), Brussels, *Revue Internationale de Philoso-*

phie. (Forthcoming); [2011]: Matthieu Fontaine, Marie-Hélène Gorisse et Shahid Rahman, « Dynamique Dialogique : Lecture d'une controverse entre logiciens jaïns et grammairiens en Inde classique », in *Kairos, revista de filosofia & ciência vol.2*, http://kairos.fc.ul.pt/, Olga Pombo & Nuno Melim (Eds.), Lisbonne; [2011]: "To Be is To Be Chosen – A Dialogical Understanding of Ontological Commitment" (with Matthieu Fontaine), in *Logic of Knowledge. Theory and Applications*, C. Bares Gomez, S. Magniez et F. Salguero (eds.), col. Dialogues and Games of Logic, Sh. Rahman, N. Clerbout et M. Fontaine (eds.), College Publication, London (submitted); [2010]: "Fiction, Creation and Fictionality – An Overview" (with Shahid Rahman), Revue *Méthodos*, n° 10 "Penser la fiction", Lille [http://methodos.revues.org/]; [2009]: "Etre et Etre choisi, Vers une logique dynamique de la fiction" (with Juan Redmond and Shahid Rahman), on line publication, stl.recherche.univ-lille3.fr/textesenligne/etre_et_etre_choisi.pdf; [2008]: *Logique Dialogique : une introduction – Première partie : Méthode de dialogique : règles et exercices* (with Juan Redmond), col. Cahiers de logique et d'épistémologie, Vol. 5, D. Gabbay & Sh. Rahman Eds., College Publications, London.

fontaine.matthieu@gmail.com

English corrections:

Victoria Magariños lectures in English at the National University of Cuyo in Mendoza (Argentina) and is a translation editor. She holds a MA degree in English Teaching from the University of Leeds (UK) and is currently working on a PhD in Linguistics at the University of Cuyo.

victoria@sourceandtarget.com

Bibliography

Aho T. & Pietarinen A.V. [2006]: *Truth and Games. Essays in Honour of Gabriel Sandu*, Acta Philosophica Fennica, Helsinki.

Anderson, A. / Belnap, N. D. [1975]. *Entailment the logic of Relevance and Necessity*. Princeton: Princeton U. Press, 1975, vol. 1.

Barth E. M. & Krabbe E. C. W. [1982]: *From Axiom to Dialogue. A Philosophical Study of Logic and Argumentation*, de Gruyter, Berlin.

Bencivenga E. [1983]: "Free Logics". In D. M. Gabbay and F. Guenthner (eds.), *Handbook of Philosophical Logic*, Vol. III, D. Reidel, Dordrecht. pp. 373-426.

Blackburn P. [2000]: "Representation, Reasoning, and Relational Structures: a Hybrid Logic Manifesto" *Logic Journal of the IGPL* , 8(3), 339-625.

Blackburn P. [2001]: "Modal logic as dialogical logic", in S. Rahman & H. Rückert (2001b), pp. 57-93.

Blass A. [1992]: "A Game Semantics for Linear Logic" in *Annals of Pure and Applied Logic*, 56, pp. 183-220.

Blass A. [1998]: "Some Semantical Aspects of Linear Logic", *J. Interest Group in Pure and Applied Logic*, 5, pp. 115-126.

Clerbout N. [2011]: "Dialogues for First-Order-Logic and Tableaux", Communication at the Workshop for Logic, Methodology and Philosophy of Science, Nancy, July 2011.

Clerbout, N. / Keiff, L. / Rahman, S.: Dialogues and Natural Deduction. In G. Primiero and S. Rahman (ed.) *Acts of Knowledge, History, Philosophy, Logic*. G. Primiero (ed.), London : College Publications. chapter 4.

Dunn, M. [1976]. Intuitive Semantics for First-Degree-Entailments and Coupled-Trees. *Philosophical Studies* 1976, 29, 149-168.

Dyckhoff R. / Francez N. [2007]. A note on harmony. Typescript, August 2007.

Felscher, W.[1985]. Dialogues as a foundation for intuitionistic logic. In D. Gabbay, D. and F. Guenthner, (editors), *Handbook of Philosophical Logic*, Volume 3, Dordrecht: Kluwer, 341–372, 1985.

Fiutek, V. / Rückert, H. / Rahman, S. [2010] *A Dialogical Semantics for Bonanno's System of Belief Revision*. To appear in *Constructions* . P. Bour et alii (ed.), London : College Publications, 2010.

Fontaine, M. / Redmond, J. [2008]. *Logique Dialogique: une introduction, Volume 1: Méthode de Dialogue: Règles et Exercices*. London : College Publications, London, 2008.

Fontaine, Matthieu & Gorisse, Marie-Hélène & Rahman, Shahid. [2011] « Dynamique Dialogique : Lecture d'une controverse entre logiciens jaïns et grammairiens en Inde classique », in *Kairos, revista de filosofia & ciência vol.2*, http://kairos.fc.ul.pt/, Olga Pombo & Nuno Melim (Eds.), Lisbonne

Genot, E. [2009a]. The Game of Enquiry: The interrogative Approach to Enquiry and Belief. *Synthese*, 2009, vol. 171/2, 271-289.

Genot, E. [2009b] Extensive Questions: From Research Agendas to Interrogative Games. Logic and its applications (LNAI 5378), 2009, 131-145.

Genot, E. [2009c]. The Game of Enquiry. PHD-Thesis, 2009, University of Lille.

Genot, E. J. / Rahman, S. [2010], Interrogative Dialogues. A (Dialogically Inspired) Game-Theoretic Semantics for Hintikka's Interrogative Tableaux, Paper presented at the 3rd World Congress on Universal Logic, Lisbon, April 2010.

Gentzen, G. [1969]. *The Collected Papers of Gerhard Gentzen*, tr. M. Szabo. Amsterdam: North-Holland 1969.

Gentzen, G. 'Investigations concerning logical deduction', trans. in Gentzen 1969, 68-131.

Girard J.Y. [1999]: "On the meaning of logical rules I: syntax vs. semantics", *Computational Logic*, in Berger and Schwichtenberg (eds.), Springer, Heidelberg, pp. 215-272.

Haas G. [1980]: "Hypothesendialoge, konstrucktiver Sequenzenkalkül une die Rechtfertigung von Dialograhmenregeln", in *Theorie des wissenschaftlichen Argumentierens*, Suhrkamp Verlag, Frankfurt.

Hintikka, J. [1999]. *Inquiry as Inquiry: A Logic of Scientific Discovery*. Dordrecht: Kluwer.

Hintikka, J., / Sandu, G., [1989]. Informational Independence as a Semantical Phenomenon. In *Logic, Methodology and Philosophy of Science*, vol. 8, J. E. Fenstad, I. T. Frolov, and R. Hilpinen (editors.), Amsterdam: Elsevier, 571–589, 1989.

Hintikka, J., Halonen, I., and Mutanen, A. [1999]. Interrogative Logic as a General Theory of Reasoning. In Hintikka 1999, pages 47–90.

Hoepelman, J. Ph. / Hoof, AJ.M., 1988. The Success of Failure. In *Proceedings of COLING, Budapest*, Budapest 1988, 250-55.

Keiff L. [2004]: "Heuristique formelle et logiques modales non normales" in *Philosophia Scientiae* , vol. 8-2, pp. 39-59, Paris, Kimé.

Keiff L. [2009]: „Dialogical Logic", text on line: *Stanford Encyclopedia of Philosophy*.

Keiff, L. [2004]. Introduction à la dialogique modale et hybride. *Philosophia Scientiae*, vol. 8-2, 89-105, 2004.

Keiff, L. [2007]. Approches dynamiques à l'argumentation formelle. PHD thesis, Lille : Université de Lille, 2007.

Keiff, L. / Rahman, S. [2010]. La Dialectique entre logique et rhétorique. *Revue de Métaphysique et Morale*, Avril-June 2010, vol. 2, 149-178.

Lorenz K. [1961]: *Arithmetik und Logik als Spiele*, Diss, Kiel.

Lorenz K. [2001]: "Basin Objectives of Dialogue Logic in Historical Perspective", in S. Rahman & H. Rückert [2001b], pp. 255-263.

Lorenz, K. [2001] Basic objectives of dialogue logic in historical perspective. *Synthese*, , vol. 127: 255–263.

Lorenzen P. / Lorenz K [1978]. *Dialogische Logik*. Darmstadt: Wissenschaftliche Buchgesellschaft, 1978.

Lorenzen P. [1955]: *Einführung in die operative Logik und Mathematik*, Springer, Berlin, Göttingen, Heidelberg.

Lorenzen P. [1958]: "Logik und Agon", *Arti del XII Congresso Internationale de Filosofia*, Venezia. pp. 187–194. (Reprinted in Lorenzen and Lorenz [1978].)

Lorenzen P. and Lorenz K. [1978]: *Dialogische Logik*. WBG, Darmstadt.

Perelman C. & Olbrechts-Tyteca L. [1958]: *La Nouvelle Rhétorique*, PUF, Paris.

Prakken H. [2005]: "Coherence and flexibility in dialogue games for argumentation". *Journal of Logic and Computation*, 15, pp. 1009-1040.

Prawitz, D [1979]. Proofs and the meaning and completeness of the logical constants. In J. Hintikka, I. Niiniluoto, and E. Saarinen (editors), *Essays on Mathematical and Philosophical Logic*, Dordrecht: Reidel, 1979, 25–40.

Prawitz, D. [1965]. *Natural Deduction*. Stockholm: Almqvist & Wiksell 1965.

Priest, G. [2001]. *An Introduction to Non-Classical Logic*. Cambridge: Cambridge U. Press, 2001.

Priest, G. [2010]. Realism, Antirealism and Consistency. In G. Primiero and S. Rahman (editors), *(Anti)Realism. The Realism-Antirealism Debate in the Age of Alternative Logics*. Forthcoming, 2010.

Rahman S. & Carnielli W. A. [2000]: "The Dialogical Approach to Paraconsistency". *Synthese*, 125, No. 1-2. pp. 201-232.

Rahman S. & Keiff L. [2004]: "On how to be a dialogician". In D. Vanderveken (Ed.) *Logic, Thought and Action*, Springer, Dordrecht, pp. 359-408.

Rahman S. & Rückert H. [2001a]: "Dialogical Connexive Logic" in S. Rahman & H. Rückert [2001b], pp. 105-139.

Rahman S. & Rückert H. [2001b]: "New Perspectives in Dialogical Logic", special issue of *Synthese*, 127.

Rahman S. & Tulenheimo T. [2006]: "From Games to Dialogues and Back: Towards a General Frame for Validity", O. Majer/A. Pietarinen/T. Tulenheimo (ed.), *Games: Unifying Logic, Language and Philosophy*, Part III, LEUS, Springer, Dordrecht.

Rahman S. & van Bendegem J.P. [2002]: "The dialogical dynamics of adaptive paraconsistency". In A. Carnielli, M. Coniglio, I. M. Loffredo D'Ottaviano (eds.), Paraconsistency, the dialogical way to the inconsistent, Marcel Dekker, New York. pp. 295-sq.

Rahman S. [1993]: *Ueber Dialogue Protologische Kategorien und andere Seltenheiten*, Peter Lang, Frankfurt, pp. 88-107.

Rahman S. [2001]: "On Frege's Nightmare. A Combination of Intuitionistic, Free and Paraconsistent Logics". In H. Wansing (ed.), *Essays on Non-Classical Logic*, World Scientific, New Jersey, London, Singapore, Hong Kong, pp. 61-85.

Rahman S. [2002]: " *Non-normal Dialogics for a wonderful world and more* " to appear in *Philosophical Insights into Logic and Mathematics*, G. Heinzmann (ed.), LEUS, Springer, Dordrecht.

Rahman S. [2004]: *Dialogique Standard: Notions fondamentales*, texte en ligne: http://stl.recherche.univ-lille3.fr/sitespersonnels/rahman/rahmancourscadre4.html

Rahman S., Damien L. & Gorisse M.H. [2004]: " La dialogique temporelle ou Patrick Blackburn par lui même".

Rahman, S. [2009]. A non normal logic for a wonderful world and more. In J. van Benthem et alia *The Age of Alternative Logics*, chez Dordrecht: Kluwer-Springer, 311-334, 2009.

Rahman, S. / Clerbout, N. / Keiff, L. [2009]. Dialogues and Natural Deduction. *Acts of Knowledge, History, Philosophy, Logic*. G. Primiero (ed.), London : College Publications, 301-336.

Rahman, S. [2011] Negation in the Logic of First Degree Entailment and Tonk. A Dialogical Study. In G. Primiero et alii (ed.). In (Anti)Realism. The Realism-Realism Debate in the Age of Alternative Logics. Dordrecht: Springer, 175-202.

Read S. [1994]:*Thinking about logic. Oxford*, Oxford University Press.

Read, S. [2000]. Harmony and autonomy in classical logic. *Journal of Philosophical Logic*, 2000, 29, 123–154.

Read, S. [2005]. The unity of the fact. Philosophy, 2005, 80, 317–42.

Read, S. [2008]. Harmony and modality. In C. D´egremont, L. Kieff, and H. Rückert (editors), *Dialogues, Logics and Other Strange Things: Essays in Honour of Shahid Rahman*, London: College Publications, 2008, 285–303.

Read, S. [2010]. General Elimination Harmony and the Meaning of the Logical Constants. Typescript, March 2010.

Redmond J. & Fontaine M. [2008]: *Logique Dialogique : une introduction, Volume 1 : Méthode de Dialogique : Règles et Exercices,* dans Cahiers de logique et Épistémologie N°5, London, College Publications, 2008. (ISBN 978-1-904987-94-9)

Restall G. [2000]: *An Introduction to Substructural Logics* , Routledge, Oxford.

Restall G. [2002]: "Carnap's Tolerance, Meaning and Logical Pluralism", Journal of Philosophy, 99, 426–443.

Rott, H.: Nonmonotonic Conditional Logic for Belief Revision. Part I: Semantics and Logic. In Proceedings of the Workshop on Nonmonotonic Reasoning, 1989, GMD Arbeitspapier 443, 45-51.

Rückert, H. [2001]. Why Dialogical Logic? In H. Wansing (ed.), *Essays on Non-Classical Logic*, N. Jersey, London ...: World Scientific, 2001, 165-185.

Rückert, H. [2007]. Dialogues as a dynamic framework for logic. PHD-Thesis, Leyden, 2007. Online in:

Rückert, H. [2011]. The Conception of Validity in Dialogical Logic. Talk at the workshop Proofs and Dialogues, Tübingen, organized by the Wilhelm-Schickard Institut für Informatik (Universität Tübingen), 25-27 February 2011.

Saarinen E. [1978]: "Dialogue Semantics versus Game-Theoretical Semantics". In *Proceedings of the Biennial Meeting of the Philosophy of Science Association* (PSA), Vol. 2: *Symposia and Invited Papers*. The University of Chicago Press, 41-59.

Schröder-Heister [2008]. P. Lorenzen's operative justification of intuitionistic logic. In M. van Atten, P. Boldini, M. Bourdeau, G. Heinzmann (eds.), *One Hundred Years of Intuitionism* (1907-2007), Basel: Birkhäuser 2008.

Stegmueller W. [1964]: "Remarks on the completeness of logical systems relative to the validity of concepts of P. Lorenzen and K. Lorenz". *Notre Dame Journal of Formal Logic*, 5, pp. 81-112.

Sundholm, B. G. [1983a]. Constructions, proofs and the meaning of the logical constants. *Journal of Philosophical Logic*, Vol. 12, 151-72.

Sundholm, B. G. [1983b]. Systems of deduction', chapter I:2 in: Gabbay, D., and F. Guenthner, *Handbook of Philosophical Logic*, Vol. I, Reidel, Dordrecht.

Sundholm, B. G. [2010]. Proofs as Acts and Proofs as Objects: Some Questions for Dag Prawitz. *Theoria*, forthcoming.

Toulmin S. [1958]: *The Uses of Argument*. Cambridge University Press, Cambridge.

Tulenheimo, T. [2009]. Independence Friendly Logic. Entry in the Stanford Encyclopaedia of Philosophy, 2009:

Tulenheimo, T. [2010]. 'On the dialogical approach to semantics'. Talk at the Workshop Amsterdam/Lille: *Dialogues and Games: Historical Roots and Contemporary Models*, 8-9 February 2010, Lille. Online inhttp://www.tulenheimo.webs.com/talks.html)

Wansing, H. [2001]. Negation. In L. Goble (editors.), *The Blackwell Guide to Philosophical Logic*, ch. 19. Oxford: Blackwell, 2001.

Wittgenstein L., [1953]: *Philosophical Investigations*, Oxford, Blackwell Publishing.

Woods J., Irvine A. & Walton D. [2000]: *Argument: Critical Thinking Logic and The Fallacies*, Prentice-Hall, Toronto.